Virgil *Aene*

The following titles are available from Bloomsbury for the OCR specifications in Latin and Greek for examinations from June 2021 to June 2023

Catullus: A Selection of Poems, with introduction, commentary notes and vocabulary by John Godwin

Cicero *Pro Cluentio*: A Selection, with introduction, commentary notes and vocabulary by Matthew Barr

Livy *History of Rome* I: A Selection, with introduction, commentary notes and vocabulary by John Storey

Ovid *Heroides*: A Selection, with introduction, commentary notes and vocabulary by Christina Tsaknaki

Tacitus *Annals* IV: A Selection, with introduction, commentary notes and vocabulary by Robert Cromarty

Virgil *Aeneid* XII: A Selection, with introduction, commentary notes and vocabulary by James Burbidge

OCR Anthology for Classical Greek AS and A Level, covering the prescribed texts by Aristophanes, Homer, Plato, Plutarch, Sophocles and Thucydides, with introduction, commentary notes and vocabulary by Simon Allcock, Sam Baddeley, John Claughton, Alastair Harden, Sarah Harden, Carl Hope and Jo Lashly

Supplementary resources for these volumes can be found at
www.bloomsbury.com/OCR-editions-2021-2023
Please type the URL into your web browser and follow the instructions to access the Companion Website. If you experience any problems, please contact Bloomsbury at academicwebsite@bloomsbury.com

Virgil *Aeneid* XII:
A Selection

Lines 1–106, 614–952

With introduction, commentary notes and
vocabulary by James Burbidge

BLOOMSBURY ACADEMIC

LONDON · NEW YORK · OXFORD · NEW DELHI · SYDNEY

BLOOMSBURY ACADEMIC
Bloomsbury Publishing Plc
50 Bedford Square, London, WC1B 3DP, UK
1385 Broadway, New York, NY 10018, USA

BLOOMSBURY, BLOOMSBURY ACADEMIC and the Diana logo
are trademarks of Bloomsbury Publishing Plc

First published in Great Britain 2020

Cover design: Terry Woodley
Cover image © PHAS/UIG via Getty Images

A catalogue record for this book is available from the British Library.

A catalog record for this book is available from the Library of Congress.

ISBN: PB: 978-1-3500-5921-4
       ePDF: 978-1-3500-5923-8
       eBook: 978-1-3500-5922-1

Typeset by RefineCatch Limited, Bungay, Suffolk
Printed and bound in India

To find out more about our authors and books visit www.bloomsbury.com
and sign up for our newsletters.

Contents

Preface

This volume is designed to guide any student who has mastered Latin up to GCSE level and wishes to read part of Book XII of Virgil's *Aeneid* in the original. The edition is, however, particularly designed to support students who are reading Virgil's text in preparation for OCR's AS/A Level Latin examination in June 2021–June 2023. Please note this edition uses AS to refer indiscriminately to AS and the first year of A Level, i.e. Group 1.

The *Aeneid* is the greatest work of Latin literature, and Book XII is one of the finest in the poem. The final three hundred or so lines are particularly rich and rewarding. My main aim in this edition is to give students some fundamental tools with which they may begin to understand and appreciate this marvellous text.

The edition contains an Introduction which situates *Aeneid* XII in the context of Virgil's life and career, and in the context of the history of the first century BC; it also explains the narrative background to this final Book of the epic, and considers some central literary aspects of the prescribed sections. The Introduction continues with a discussion of some of the linguistic challenges facing the reader new to Virgil's poetry, and of the metre; it concludes with some recommendations for further reading.

The Commentary Notes which follow the Text aim to help students bridge the gap between GCSE and AS or A Level Latin. Their focus is therefore primarily linguistic, with particular attention given to points of grammar, idiom and word order which seem likely to challenge students at this level. They also aim to make clear what is happening in the narrative or what a speaker is saying (neither of which are always obvious at first sight), and to clarify any references to events or persons mentioned earlier in the poem (since *Aeneid* XII is the last

Book of the epic, there are a lot of these). At the end of the book is a full vocabulary list, including all the words contained in the prescribed sections; words in OCR's Defined Vocabulary List for AS Level Latin are indicated by an asterisk.

I am very grateful to Alice Wright for suggesting that I write this book, and for her patience, good humour and support (and that of her team at Bloomsbury) throughout its gestation. I am also grateful to Tonbridge School for offering a supportive environment in which to write, and for enabling me to spend an inspirational two weeks in Lazio early in 2018 to kick-start my work. Writing for a student readership has reminded me of my own time as a student, and of some of the teachers I have been lucky to have at various stages – particularly my schoolteachers Aubs Scrase, Keith Louis and Brian Boothroyd (with whom I first read Virgil), and my college tutor Peta Fowler (with whom I first studied *Aeneid* XII). Lastly, thanks and much love to Philippa, Robin and Patrick, who have put up with absences and grumpiness along the way.

James Burbidge
Tonbridge, June 2019

Introduction

Virgil's life and career

Virgil lived in the first century BC, during one of the best-documented periods of ancient history. We know a lot about the world in which he grew up and wrote his poems; reliable information about his own life is, however, in short supply. Virgil writes little about himself in his surviving poetry, and contemporary records are scarce. But the bare bones of a biography can be put together.

The poet seems to have been born in 70 BC. He grew up in what is now northern Italy, in the vicinity of the town of Mantua. This town lies just north of the river Po, on the eastern side of the great plain between the Alps and the Apennines (an area known at the time of Virgil's birth as *Gallia Cisalpina*, 'Gaul on this side of the Alps').

The earliest securely attested event in Virgil's life is the publication of his first collection of verse, the *Eclogues*. This took place during the 30s BC, most probably towards the beginning of that decade. The *Eclogues* are a collection of ten poems (between 63 and 111 lines long), in the pastoral genre. Set in rural locations, these poems mostly portray herdsmen or other countrymen talking, to one another or to themselves, about a variety of subjects – sometimes trivial, but often serious (love, home, exile, politics, time, death).

Soon after the publication of the *Eclogues*, Virgil seems to have entered the circle of Maecenas, the aristocratic literary patron who was very close to Octavian (the future emperor Augustus: see the next section). We know little of his subsequent activities in the 30s BC (although vignettes survive in the poetry of his contemporary and friend Horace: *Satires* I.5 and I.6). He lived during much of this period near Neapolis, the city now known as Napoli. At least some of

his time will have been spent in the composition of his next work, the
Georgics.

The *Georgics* is a poem about agriculture and farming, a little over
two thousand lines in length. It is made up of four 'books' or sections:
the first is concerned with arable farming, the second with growing
vines and trees, the third with the rearing of livestock and the fourth
with bees. These books are didactic in form: that is, they ostensibly
offer teaching and guidance to their readers. Alongside technical
information, the poem presents sustained reflection on contemporary
historical events as well as on timeless themes such as the relationship
between humans and the earth, work, love, sex and death.

The *Georgics* is dedicated to Maecenas and was published in 29 BC.
This masterpiece – hailed by the poet and critic John Dryden in the
seventeenth century as simply 'the best poem by the best poet' –
established Virgil as the foremost Latin poet of an exceptional
generation (his rough contemporaries included Horace, Varius Rufus,
Propertius, Tibullus and Gallus).

At some point in the 30s or early 20s BC, Virgil decided to embark
upon an epic poem. The *Aeneid* must have taken up much of his time
during the 20s; fragments of letters from this period show that the
work was at times very challenging. The epic was eagerly awaited
during the period of its composition: 'make way, Roman writers, make
way, you Greeks! – something greater than the *Iliad* is coming to birth',
said Propertius (II.34.65–6). When it finally appeared, the *Aeneid* not
only confirmed Virgil's reputation as the finest poet of his own
generation – it was quickly recognized as the greatest work of Latin
literature and as the national epic (a status it was to retain throughout
antiquity). The poem seems to have been substantially complete when
the poet died in 19 BC, but the presence of incomplete lines (631n.)
indicates that the finishing touches had not yet been applied. Indeed,
there is a story that Virgil had ordered the poem to be burned, but that
this was forbidden by the emperor Augustus – the poem was instead

handed over to Virgil's friends Varius Rufus and Plotius Tucca to be edited for publication.

Historical background and context

The era in which Virgil lived was one of the most tumultuous in Roman and, indeed, European history. Awareness of some of the main historical developments which took place during these years can help us to understand certain features of his poetry. To that end, we shall here look at three processes central to the history of the first century BC: the growth of the Roman empire, the collapse of the Republican system of government, and the establishment of the Principate under Augustus.

During the four centuries before Virgil was born, the city-state of Rome in central Italy had risen from relatively humble beginnings to become the most effective military power the ancient world had ever seen. Roman forces had first overwhelmed the other peoples of Italy, then the western Mediterranean, then much of the eastern Mediterranean world. Not only had Roman armies conquered the peoples of these areas, but the Roman state had also seized control of their territory and gone on to govern (and exploit) it as an empire. During Virgil's lifetime, this empire continued to grow: Rome's conquest of the eastern Mediterranean was completed by Pompey's campaigns in the 60s BC and the later annexation of Egypt in 30 BC, and with Julius Caesar's conquest of Gaul in the 50s BC her power expanded into northern Europe. The acquisition and maintenance of control over so great an empire required a huge military commitment from the Roman state. By the first century BC, the Roman army was fully professional. Many of Rome's leading generals were also politicians. For large numbers of Romans, military service and warfare were a way of life.

The expansion of the Roman empire had been achieved under the 'Republican' system of government. The origins of this arrangement were placed by the Romans in the sixth century BC; it had evolved over subsequent centuries into a complex political system, in which power was shared by different elements within the state. Male citizens annually elected representatives (who were mostly aristocrats) to hold political and military offices, usually for specified periods of time; these representatives became part of the senate, which was the main decision-making body in the state. When functioning optimally, this arrangement gave all classes a stake in the activities of the state and was thus conducive to social harmony. It certainly proved resilient and effective for a very long time. But, for a variety of reasons (many connected to the growth of Rome's empire), from the mid-second century BC onwards this 'Republican' system was put under increasing pressure. The authority of the senate declined as individual military commanders acquired unprecedented wealth, influence and power. Friction between these commanders, or between commanders and the senate, became increasingly violent, and exploded into full-scale civil war on at least three occasions during the first century BC. The most significant of these civil wars was that fought in 49–45 BC between Julius Caesar and the forces of the senate, led by Pompey the Great; for soon after winning victory Caesar was declared Dictator, and in effect autocracy replaced the 'Republican' system. Although Caesar was assassinated in 44 BC, in practice that system would never again fully be revived.

The aftermath of Caesar's murder was chaotic. His assassins had hoped to reinstate the 'Republican' system, but they were thwarted by the Caesarian faction – led by Mark Antony and Lepidus (two of Caesar's closest allies) and the nineteen-year-old Octavian (Caesar's great-nephew and adopted son and heir). A further civil war now broke out, with massive-scale mobilization of troops (it has been estimated that over a quarter of all male citizens aged between seventeen and forty-six were involved in this struggle). In 42 BC, at Philippi in northern Greece, the assassins' army was defeated by the Caesarians; losses were enormous (approximately twenty thousand dead on each side). The Caesarian faction now controlled the Roman state, and its leaders attempted to restore some stability to the empire. The eastern Mediterranean had suffered much disruption during the 40s, and Antony was tasked with setting affairs there in order; Octavian remained at Rome and supervised the empire in the west, while Lepidus took responsibility for North Africa. But harmony between the three men did not last. Lepidus was increasingly marginalized, and removed from power in 36 BC; Antony and Octavian quarrelled repeatedly throughout the 30s, and eventually turned to armed conflict to settle their differences. This conflict reached its climax in 31 BC, with the decisive defeat of Antony's navy by Octavian's at Actium in western Greece; the following year, Octavian's forces invaded Egypt and Antony committed suicide, leaving Octavian in sole control of the Roman world.

Over the next few years, Octavian devised a new arrangement for the government of that world. In appearance, it was not so different from the 'Republican' system: decisions were made by the senate, elections were held, the rule of law restored; it was possible to claim that traditional government had been reinstated. In practice, however, Octavian continued to hold overwhelming military power as well as certain political offices, giving him a dominant role in the state and enormous influence over other elements within it. The system of government he created, with its 'Republican' appearance and autocratic core, is nowadays known as the 'Principate' (*princeps*, or 'leader', was one of the terms Octavian adopted to denote his position). The system was refined over time, but initially established in 27 BC: at that time, the title *Augustus* (meaning something like 'the revered one') was bestowed upon Octavian by the senate, recognizing his special position within the state. The political arrangement he had created would prove extremely durable, lasting (with modifications) for five centuries or so. Augustus was the first Roman emperor.

Approaching the *Aeneid*

As we have seen, at some point in the 30s or early 20s BC Virgil seems to have made a decision to embark upon an epic poem. It is possible that early in the planning stages the poet had considered writing directly about recent history, as some earlier Roman epic poets had done: for at the beginning of *Georgic* III, he announces (in rather elusive terms) a plan to write what sounds like a poem in honour of Octavian. But if Virgil had ever seriously contemplated such a work (and this is open to doubt), he certainly changed his mind. The epic which he went on to compose – although it contained some passages dealing with recent events and, indeed, with Augustus himself – took its main subject matter not from history but from myth.

The story which Virgil chose to tell was that of the Trojan prince Aeneas – a warrior (and son of the goddess Venus) who had survived the fall of Troy to the Greek army led by Agamemnon, and had become the leader of a community of Trojan refugees in exile. Virgil did not invent this character. Aeneas has a (fairly minor) role in the earliest surviving – and greatest – work of Greek poetry, Homer's *Iliad*; already there the god Poseidon knows that Aeneas is destined to survive the war and lead the Trojans thereafter (*Il.* XX.300–8). Various accounts of Aeneas' movements in exile are found in subsequent Greek literature: some texts have him remaining in the Troad or the Aegean, but others see him wandering into the western Mediterranean. By the third century BC, Aeneas was particularly linked with central Italy. This connection was taken up by early Roman historians and poets, writing in the third and second centuries BC. From surviving fragments of their work, it is clear that the coming of Aeneas to Latium was regarded as part of national mythology: the details of the story vary, but Aeneas is usually said to have founded the city of Lavinium and to have been an ancestor of Romulus, the founder of Rome.

Virgil had chosen, then, to write about a central figure in Roman myth – a figure who could be considered as the founder if not of the city of Rome itself then of the people who would one day be regarded as Romans (this is certainly how Virgil sees Aeneas: *Aeneid* I.1–7, I.33; XII.827, 838–40). Aeneas was thus a character who would have been familiar to Virgil's first readers; but his story had never been told with the detail and on the scale that Virgil would use. For Virgil modelled his *Aeneid* on the *Iliad* and *Odyssey* of Homer – poems universally acknowledged in antiquity as the finest achievements of Greek or Roman literature, which presented their heroic stories with considerable amplitude. (The *Iliad* is over fifteen thousand lines long, the *Odyssey* over twelve thousand lines; the *Aeneid* contains just under ten thousand lines).

Virgil decided to devote the first half of his epic (Books I–VI) to the wanderings of Aeneas as he makes his way from Troy to central Italy; the second half (Books VII–XII) deals with the arrival of the Trojans in Italy and the war they fight there against the people of Latium. Some elements incorporated into his plot were already present in previous treatments of Aeneas; these are supplemented by material invented by Virgil, material which is often inspired by other literature (and especially by Homer).

Aeneid VII–XII: The war in Italy

The second half of the *Aeneid* has in modern times tended to be less highly valued than the first half. But Virgil's own view was rather different, as is clear from some lines early in Book VII which introduce his martial theme:

I shall speak of fearsome wars,
I shall speak of battle-lines and of kings driven to their deaths by their
    courage,
Of a band of men from Etruria and of the whole land of Hesperia
    [= Italy]
Forced to take up arms. For me this is the birth of a higher order of
    things;
This is a greater work I now set in motion.

(VII.41–5)

War was traditionally considered by the ancients the grandest
subject matter for a work of literature, and the last line here clearly
shows that the poet regards the second half of his epic – the account
of the war in Italy – as grander than the first half. This theme was also
one with real contemporary resonance for Virgil's Roman readers: as
we have seen, not only were they citizens of the most successful
military power of the ancient world, they had also recently lived
through many years of brutal civil war. (The war between the Trojans
and the people of Latium can be seen as a quasi-civil war, given that
these two peoples will in the near future become one: cf. XII.819–28,
834–40.)

The course of the war itself is, roughly, as follows. (This summary
aims to include those events in the second half of the poem which are
most important for an understanding of Book XII; Book XI is given
special attention, as it supplies the immediate background for the final
Book.)

Soon after the beginning of Book VII, the Trojans arrive by sea at
Latium in central Italy – the land which they have been trying to
reach throughout Books I–VI. Initially, they are welcomed by the
local king, Latinus. Latinus has been given warnings by the gods that
he should betroth his daughter, Lavinia, to a foreigner; and he decides
to offer Aeneas her hand in marriage, as well as land for his people.
Aeneas is delighted. But at this point, the goddess Juno (who hates

Troy and all Trojans, and has persecuted Aeneas throughout his wanderings) intervenes, sending the monstrous Fury Allecto to rouse conflict in Latium. Allecto brings about a violent uprising of the local people against the Trojans, in spite of King Latinus' protests. The Fury has a particularly powerful effect on Turnus – a prince of the Rutulian people who was himself a suitor of Lavinia (much favoured by her mother Amata, Latinus' wife) before the Trojans arrived. Turnus is roused to violent anger, and leads the uprising; many other central Italian communities send him military support.

Aeneas is deeply concerned by this turn of events. In Book VIII, he heads up the river Tiber, leaving most of his men behind in their camp as he goes in search of allies. He encounters a small community of Greek exiles who have settled at Pallanteum. Their king, Evander, welcomes Aeneas as a guest, and later supplies him with a small number of cavalry, who are led by his only son, Pallas. Evander advises Aeneas that much greater support is available from a large host of Etruscan warriors gathered at Caere. Aeneas proceeds to Caere to make this further alliance.

Book IX narrates events which take place while Aeneas is in Pallanteum and Caere. Turnus leads the people of Latium and their Italian allies against the Trojan camp near the mouth of the river. The Trojans refuse to give battle (just as Aeneas has ordered). But after a night in which the Trojans fail to get a message through to Aeneas, Turnus and his men begin a siege. Turnus fights heroically, and even manages to get inside the camp himself – but is eventually beaten back.

In Book X, Aeneas returns by sea to the Trojan camp, accompanied by his newly gained allies. They disembark onto the shore and fight a savage battle against Turnus' forces. During this battle, Pallas – the young son of Evander who has been entrusted to Aeneas – is killed by Turnus. When Aeneas learns of this, he fights with berserk rage; the goddess Juno decides to remove Turnus from the battlefield so that he will not be killed. Turnus' friend, the unpleasant Mezentius, leads the Latins in his absence: but at the end of the book Mezentius is killed by Aeneas, and the Trojans drive back their opponents.

Book XI begins with a sombre account of the funerals for those on both sides who died in the battle. Then, in Latinus' city, the king convenes a council of his people to discuss the crisis. Latinus is eager to come to terms with the Trojans, and he is supported in this position by the statesman Drances, who proposes that if Turnus insists on opposing the Trojans then he should fight Aeneas in single combat rather than risk the lives of others. Turnus urges Latinus not to give up hope of military success, but also promises that he will fight the single combat – if that is the king's will. But at this point, news arrives that the Trojans and their allies have moved onto the offensive (hitherto they have fought a defensive campaign): the council breaks up without a formal resolution as Turnus seizes the moment, ordering that the troops be armed. He arranges his forces: some are left to protect Latinus' city, the cavalry (under the warrior-princess Camilla) are drawn up on the plain in front of the city, and Turnus himself lays an ambush for Aeneas' infantry in a forest.

The cavalry of the Trojans and their allies soon approaches. The subsequent engagement is initially evenly fought; but after a period of spectacular success, Camilla is killed and her forces turn and flee: some reach the safety of Latinus' city, but many are killed on the plain. Turnus has been waiting in ambush for Aeneas; but on learning that the enemy cavalry have now reached the walls of the city, he is forced to abandon his position in order to go to help its defenders. Soon after he leaves, Aeneas' infantry pass through the place Turnus has been watching and advance on the city. Evening now falls, with the Trojans and their allies camped around Latinus' city – faced by its defenders, some of whom camp outside the walls.

Aeneid XII: A summary of the plot

Turnus realizes that the men of Latium are looking to him now (1–9). He promises Latinus that he will fight Aeneas in single combat, and bids the king draw up a treaty (10–17). Latinus is reluctant to send Turnus to his death, and blames himself for the disastrous course of the war (18–45); but Turnus angrily insists that he will be able to stand up to Aeneas (45–53). Queen Amata, in tears, urges Turnus not to fight Aeneas – and says that she will kill herself rather than see Lavinia married to Aeneas (54–63). Lavinia blushes, and Turnus becomes more agitated still (64–70); he sends Idmon to propose to Aeneas that the two leaders fight in single combat the next morning (71–80). Turnus then enters the palace, calls for his horses and tries on his arms ahead of the combat (81–106).

The narrator turns away from Turnus in line 107, to show Aeneas' preparations in his camp for the duel (107–12). Virgil then describes the dawning of the next day, the arrangements for the single combat and the gathering of spectators, Trojan and Italian (113–33). The goddess Juno, who has consistently opposed the Trojans throughout the epic, sees that Turnus' end is near: she summons his divine sister, the water-nymph Juturna, and urges her to help her brother (134–60). Meanwhile, Latinus and Turnus come out onto the plain in front of Latinus' city and meet Aeneas (who is accompanied by his son Iulus): Aeneas and Latinus agree the terms of the duel, and solemn oaths are sworn to abide by this treaty (161–215).

Turnus' Rutulian soldiers are concerned that the duel will not be a contest between equals (216–21): Juturna stokes these feelings amongst all the Latins (222–43), then sends a bird-omen in the sky which the augur Tolumnius interprets as a signal that successful resistance to the Trojans is still possible (244–65). Tolumnius hurls a spear at Aeneas' supporters, killing one of his allies from Pallanteum: fighting between Trojans and Italians now breaks out anew, with

Latinus forced to flee (266–310). As Aeneas tries to restrain his men from battle, urging all to respect the treaty, he is hit by an arrow (311–23). He is forced to withdraw, and Turnus seizes this opportunity to enter the fighting himself: soon dominating the battlefield, he drives the Trojans back (324–82).

Aeneas returns to the camp, where the doctor Iapyx attempts to treat his wound: Iapyx struggles until Venus intervenes to heal her son (383–429). The Italians have advanced close to the Trojan camp (406–10); but Aeneas now re-emerges to lead his men (430–45). The Italians' advance is halted, and soon they are themselves put to flight (446–63). Aeneas wishes to fight only Turnus: but at this point Juturna disguises herself as Turnus' charioteer Metiscus (whom she has in reality knocked from his chariot) and drives her brother away from Aeneas, who is unable to reach the Rutulian; in angry frustration at Turnus' failure to keep to the treaty, the Trojan leader attacks the Italians directly (464–99).

A bloody passage of battle-narrative ensues, with Aeneas killing many Italians and Turnus many Trojans (500–53). Neither side is able decisively to gain the upper hand, until Aeneas (at Venus' suggestion) orders his men to attack Latinus' city itself (554–73). Some mount the walls to fire buildings, and others attack the gates: terror seizes the inhabitants (574–92). Seeing this, assuming that Turnus must have fallen in battle and blaming herself for the dreadful things that have happened, Queen Amata in despair takes her own life (593–603); Lavinia and Latinus are distraught, the palace rings with sounds of grief, and the news quickly spreads throughout the city (604–11).

Turnus, who is fighting some distance away, hears this noise from the city and wonders what is going on (614–22). Juturna, still disguised as Metiscus, urges him to continue fighting there (623–30); but Turnus, who has recognized his sister, tells her that he will not stand by and watch people and homes being destroyed: he is not afraid to die (631–49). Now Saces rides up, wounded, and urges Turnus to come to help – for Aeneas is attacking the city (650–64). This speech has a shattering impact on Turnus; he tells Juturna that he must go to fight Aeneas, and rushes off (665–83). He comes crashing through the battle-lines to the city walls: there he tells his men that he alone will fight, and they make way (684–96). Aeneas is delighted, and abandons his attack on the city (697–703).

All the Trojans and the Italians now lay aside their weapons and turn to watch the single combat; Latinus, too, looks on (704–9). Aeneas and Turnus cast their spears at each other, then rush to fight at close quarters with swords (710–24). Jupiter weighs the destinies of the two men in his scales (725–7). Turnus' sword-blade shatters (728–41); without a weapon he flees, pursued by Aeneas (742–65). Aeneas tries to recover his spear from the stump of a tree sacred to Faunus; the god grips it tight in response to an appeal from Turnus, until Venus tears it out for her son after Juturna has given Turnus his sword (766–87). The warriors face each other once more (788–90).

At this point, Virgil turns to focus on Jupiter and Juno, who are looking on from the sky. Jupiter accuses Juno of being behind Juturna's interventions in support of Turnus, and forbids any further interference (791–806). Juno yields to this demand, but insists that if the Trojans are to settle in Latium then their descendants must be considered Italian, not Trojan (806–28). Jupiter agrees to this, and Juno withdraws (829–42). Jupiter now sends down to Latium a Dira, as a sign to deter Juturna from further action (843–60). The Dira turns into an owl and flies at Turnus: he is unnerved (861–8), and Juturna, understanding that resistance is now futile, withdraws (869–86).

Aeneas and Turnus exchange brief speeches (888–95). Turnus attempts to hurl a large rock at Aeneas, but it falls short (896–918). Aeneas then casts his spear, which pierces Turnus' thigh (919–29). Turnus acknowledges his own defeat, and appeals to Aeneas for mercy

(930–8); the Trojan considers this, but sees that Turnus is wearing Pallas' sword-belt and is reminded of the young man's death: in rage, he plunges his sword into the chest of Turnus, who dies (939–52).

Speech, character and emotion

The first word of *Aeneid* XII is 'Turnus'; its final lines describe the moment of his death. In many ways, the Book is about Turnus: his character, his fate and his reaction to this. This is particularly true of the passages which form the AS Level set text, XII.1–106 and 614–727. These two episodes are closely related in content and structure. In both, Turnus is the central figure. The first passage, and much of the second, lack dynamic action and, indeed, much narrative; these are mostly static scenes of reflection and dialogue. Each episode begins with Turnus facing a military crisis: his army has suffered a major defeat (1–9); Latinus' city is being attacked (614–22). Turnus responds emotionally on each occasion (3–9, 620–2). There follow long central scenes of discussion and decision-making (10–80, 623–82), with Turnus and other characters speaking, in which the main issue at stake is how Turnus should respond to the crisis. In each case, Turnus proposes to fight against Aeneas in single combat (11–17, 632–49); loved ones attempt to dissuade him (19–45, 56–63), or have already tried to (625–30), but Turnus' determination only becomes greater as the scenes continue (48–53, 72–80, 676–80). Both of the central scenes end with Turnus making an abrupt departure after affirming this determination: in the first case, he goes to arm on the eve of combat (81–106); in the second, he rushes into the combat itself (681–96).

Both episodes, then, involve a great deal of direct speech. Of lines 1–106, 62 are in direct speech; of lines 614–727, 45 lines. Of the AS Level set text, 48.6 per cent is thus direct speech. This proportion is not atypical of the *Aeneid* as a whole: it has been calculated that direct speech makes up 46.75 per cent of all the lines in the poem. In fact, an abundance of direct speech is a striking feature of almost all ancient epic poetry, going back to Homer (it makes up 45 per cent of the *Iliad*, and 67 per cent of the *Odyssey*). Of course, there is some variation within the texts: not all scenes are rich in speeches. But those that are become at times very close to drama in their form. For example, of the 52 lines in the scene between Jupiter and Juno (791–842) in the A Level set text, only seven are not in direct speech; of the 71 lines in the scene at XII.10–80 (an unusually extended multiple-speaker private conversation), 56 are in direct speech. These scenes could be played on a stage.

This volume of direct speech lends a dramatic quality to the storytelling, then; it also allows for a greater depth of characterization than would otherwise be possible. What people do and what they say are the two primary means by which we assess their character: as we have seen, the *Aeneid* (and ancient epic more generally) give almost as much space to speech as they do to narrative of action. Turnus makes 29 speeches in the *Aeneid*, 12 of them in Book XII; we get to know (and judge) him through these, as much as by his deeds.

Direct speech also allows for the articulate expression of emotion. Virgil is a great poet of emotion, and Book XII forms a highly emotional climax to the *Aeneid*. Strong emotions can, of course, be conveyed in passages of narrative (consider, for example, the extraordinary XII.665–8), sometimes enhanced by special features like similes (as at XII.4–9 or 101–6, and enigmatically at 64–9). But speech is especially effective in this respect. Amata's anguish (XII.56–63), Saces' urgency (653–64), Juturna's despair (872–84), Aeneas' bitterness (889–93) and fury (947–9): in all of these cases, direct speech is used to show the intensity of feelings. This is especially true of the presentation of Turnus. Turnus' emotions run very high throughout much of the second half of the *Aeneid* – at times, indeed, raising questions about his mental stability (101–2n., 669n., 680n.);

whether this is Turnus' natural disposition or rather a legacy of Allecto's violent intervention in Book VII is left unclear by Virgil. At any rate, his speeches give us insight into his feelings: his surging anger at Aeneas and proud determination to fight (11–17, 48–53, 72–80, 95–100), his noble compassion for his comrades and bravery in going to face death (632–49, 676–80), his frightened recognition of Jupiter's hostility (894–5) and his fear as Aeneas prepares to deliver the death-blow (931–8).

The single combat

The single combat between Aeneas and Turnus forms the climax to *Aeneid* XII and, indeed, to the whole epic. In a sense, the entire second half has been building up to this point; certainly, once Turnus has killed Pallas, it is clear that Aeneas wants personal revenge. The suggestion that a single combat might settle the war is first made by Aeneas early in Book XI; after this prospect has been thrust at Turnus a number of times, he finally agrees to it in the opening scenes of Book XII. But even then, and despite elaborate preparations, the combat is delayed as a result of Juturna's intervention, Aeneas' wounding and Turnus' re-entry into battle. Only after Aeneas has attacked Latinus' city does Turnus fulfil his promise to fight the Trojan leader.

The account of the single combat begins in earnest at XII.710, after lines 684–709 have set the scene; it continues until the end of the Book at line 952 (albeit with a substantial break for the scene between Jupiter and Juno, to which we shall return). Thus, it straddles both the AS Level and A Level set texts. The length of the passage reflects its importance as the climax of the poem.

The combat can be seen as having three phases. The first phase (710–41) contains the great majority of the actual fighting: an initial exchange of spear-casts, followed by ferocious fighting at close quarters; this comes to an end when Turnus' sword shatters. In the second phase (742–90), Turnus flees from Aeneas: he is unable to get away from the battlefield, but outruns his pursuer. Aeneas eventually recovers his spear with the help of Venus, and Juturna gives Turnus his favoured sword; the two warriors then move to confront each other again. (Jupiter now intervenes to detach first Juno and then Juturna from their support for Turnus: 791–886.) The third and final phase (887–952) involves only a few actions, but they are decisive: after a short exchange of words, Turnus fails in his attempt to hurl a rock at Aeneas; Aeneas casts his spear and hits Turnus in the thigh; he considers sparing his enemy, but overcome by emotion kills him with his sword.

The combat between the two warriors is pretty stylized. Single combat was not unknown in Roman warfare, even in the first century BC; but Virgil presents the fighting between Aeneas and Turnus in a manner which often owes more to literary convention and his own imagination than to any attempt to produce a strictly realistic portrayal of combat. The clash lasts a very long time, mainly because there is an implausibly long chase during it; the characters speak to each other during the struggle; most notably, all of the other fighters on the battlefield stop fighting and stand (or sit) to watch Aeneas and Turnus. This stylization may at first strike us as rather unconvincing. But we are quite familiar with stylized combat in modern art, especially in film: there, we are usually happy to ignore unrealistic or even implausible elements in the portrayal of fighting, provided that we recognize the (unrealistic) conventions that are being followed. We should apply a similar approach to *Aeneid* XII.

Aeneas' killing of Turnus at the end of the single combat is the most discussed and most controversial scene in the epic. Most of the debate has focused on whether this killing is just, or at least justifiable – and if so, why, or if not, why not. The issues involved are not simple. This is not a murder, but a battlefield killing; our response to it will depend on what we think about this war, perhaps even what we think about war more generally. The killing is presented as an act of vengeance; our feelings about this will be guided by how we judge Turnus' behaviour earlier in the poem, and by our view of the ethics of revenge. Aeneas acts not in cold blood, but aflame with rage; the *Aeneid* is profoundly interested in the relationship between reason and emotion, which also fascinated ancient philosophers: a range of responses to Aeneas' action is again possible, depending on one's position. A killing forms the climax of the poem, as is also the case in the *Iliad* and the *Odyssey*; perhaps our response to Aeneas will owe something to what we think of Achilles' killing of Hector and Odysseus' killing of the suitors. And for Virgil's first readers, an act of revenge on a battlefield for the killing of a loved one had significant contemporary resonance: Octavian/Augustus had risen to prominence as an avenger of the assassination of his adoptive father, Julius Caesar; what we make of him may affect what we think of Aeneas. At any rate, there are many prisms through which the final scene of the *Aeneid* can be viewed – and you must come to your own conclusions about it. The one thing that is certain is that by choosing to end his whole poem with the moment of Turnus' death, Virgil encourages us to dwell upon it: the extraordinarily bold, abrupt ending offers us no comfortable answers to the questions it raises. It is one of the great closures in world literature.

The gods in *Aeneid* XII

The role of divinities in observing, and at times actively participating in, events in the mortal world is one of the most striking features of most ancient epic poetry from Homer onwards. The involvement of the divine emphasizes the importance of the events being narrated, and allows perspectives on the action which may not be accessible to the mortal characters to be opened up.

In *Aeneid* XII, some of the divinities involved in the narrative are involved because they have a family relationship to one of the mortals present. Juturna's actions, for example, are motivated by concern for her brother Turnus; Venus' actions, by concern for her son Aeneas. Both these divinities appear in person among the mortals and get physically involved in the action, although usually in disguise (which is not always successful: 632n.) or without being seen (XII.416-22); epiphanies, where gods appear to mortals in their proper form, are pretty rare in the *Aeneid*.

The gods with the most significant roles in *Aeneid* XII are Jupiter and Juno. They appear separately at earlier points (XII.134-60, 725-7), but their most important scene is shared (XII.791-842). As the king and queen of the Olympian gods, these are the grandest divinities of all; their involvement at the climax of the poem emphasizes the significance of the action, and adds a massive grandeur to the conclusion of the epic. Juno, the great opponent of the Trojans, finally yields to destiny – but acts to ensure that the Trojans' victory in Latium will be a qualified one (819-28n.). Jupiter's primary role throughout the *Aeneid* has been to supervise the fulfilment of fate (as we are reminded in lines 725-7); at 791-886, he aims to achieve this by detaching first Juno and then Juturna from their practical support for Turnus, so that Aeneas can gain his destined victory. Jupiter takes responsibility himself for winning over Juno; he delegates the task of dismissing Juturna to the sinister Dira (846-8n.). Such employment of subordinates as intermediaries moving between the immortal and mortal planes is an important aspect of the presentation of the major gods in the *Aeneid* (compare Juno's employment of Juturna earlier in Book XII); it gives the grandest Olympian divinities a way of affecting human affairs while retaining their dignity and their distance.

When a god helps a mortal to achieve something in ancient epic, this should not be seen as detracting in any way from that mortal's achievement. Indeed, if anything, the fact that a divinity is prepared to lend a mortal support is considered within the world of epic to be a tribute to that mortal; divine help renders a man even more impressive than he would be otherwise.

Style: Simile, metaphor, hyperbole and sound

The style of the *Aeneid* – how Virgil says what he says – is important to its effectiveness as a poem. Here we shall briefly consider four aspects of this style.

The most striking feature for the modern reader is probably Virgil's use of extended similes. Here the poet compares something in his story to something outside his story, often at some length (occasionally up to ten lines or so – although the norm is more like four or five lines). Similes of such length are a feature of ancient epic from Homer onwards; epics of war are particularly rich in them. For readers brought up on modern novels (which do not usually contain anything like this), extended similes can at first seem highly artificial; but once one is familiar with this convention of epic style, one can appreciate their role in enriching the texture of the narrative.

The primary function of the extended similes is to make what is happening in the story clearer and more vivid to the reader. A favoured technique is to compare something happening in the human world to something in the world of nature: thus, Turnus is compared to a hunted lion (4–8), to a bull about to fight (103–6) or to a boulder crashing down a mountainside (684–9); Aeneas and Turnus are compared to fighting bulls (715–22), or to a dog hunting a stag (749–57). Elsewhere, illustrations are taken from the human world: Lavinia's blush is compared to dyed ivory or an arrangement of flowers

(67–9), the Dira's flight to an arrow-shot (856–9) and Turnus' weakness to that of a man in a nightmare (908–12). Virgil likes to have many points of contact between the thing described in the simile and the thing in the narrative which it is illustrating: this is sometimes called the 'multiple-correspondence' technique (particularly rich examples are found at 715–22 and 749–57).

As well as extended similes, the *Aeneid* also makes use of shorter similes (740, 923) and other types of comparison (733, 764–5, 921–3) which will seem less unfamiliar to the modern reader.

Imagery more generally is an important part of epic style (although epic tends to be less rich in metaphor than, for example, lyric). Sometimes, Virgil will sustain a particular metaphor over a long period: the most notable example in *Aeneid* XII is imagery of fire and heat. Turnus 'burns' with violent passion throughout the opening scene (*ardet* 3, *accenso* 9, *ardentem* 55, *ardet* 71, *ardentis* 101); at times, image seems almost to become reality (101–2n.). He reacts to the news of Aeneas' attack on the city in a similar way (*aestuat* 666, *ardentes* 670), and he is *ardentem* early in the single combat (732). Later, it is Aeneas who is 'on fire' with rage (*accensus* 946); he and his words 'seethe' (*fervida* 894, *fervidus* 951). These metaphors give vivid expression to the emotions of the two protagonists (related imagery is used of Lavinia's blush: 64–6); they also serve to raise the temperature of the narrative and to show that the action is 'hotting up' (Juno is said to have 'inflamed' the war: *accendere* 804). Closely connected is imagery of ice and cold: as Turnus weakens, his blood freezes 'icy with cold' (*gelidus concrevit frigore sanguis* 905); as he dies, his limbs are 'slackened with cold' (*solvuntur frigore* 951).

Other metaphors are not sustained in quite the same way, but do offer some striking and memorable images. The Tiber is 'hot' with spilt blood (35–6). Turnus' violent passion 'is made more ill' by Latinus' attempt to 'heal' it (46). The warriors confronting Messapus are an 'iron crop' (663–4n.). Fire billows in 'waves' (673). The wood of the olive tree holds Aeneas' spear in a 'bite' (782). Grief 'eats away at' Juno (801), and she 'rolls waves of anger' inside her breast (831); later, she 'twists her mind around' (841). Life is consistently 'light' (63, 660, 873, 935; contrast 881, 952). Sometimes Virgil will place a series of images in close proximity; such clusters can make a passage particularly evocative. Thus, within the last eight lines of *Aeneid* XII, Aeneas has 'drunk in' reminders of his grief at the death of Pallas (945); 'on fire' with anger (946), he tells Turnus that Pallas 'is sacrificing' him (948–9), as he 'buries' his sword in Turnus' chest (950), 'seething' (951); Turnus' limbs are 'slackened with cold' (951), and his life 'flees' (952).

Hyperbole is the technical rhetorical term for 'exaggeration'. This is a striking feature of Virgil's epic narrative, at least at times: the poet is careful not to over-deploy it, since naturally hyperbole becomes less effective the more often it appears. However, in the single combat at the climax of the poem, Virgil adopts a consistently grand manner – and density of hyperbole is a crucial aspect of this.

Aeneas and Turnus are presented as 'huge' (708, 927) and can seem very tall, indeed 'high' (729, 902); the simile at 701–3 goes further, comparing Aeneas' size to that of mountains. The two warriors are also 'fast' (711); then at 733, Turnus flees 'more quickly than the East Wind'. Their fighting generates loud noise (712), and here the hyperbole is especially notable: Aeneas 'thunders' with his arms (700: compare 654); the earth groans (713) and noise fills the sky (724). Later, the noise of Aeneas' decisive spear-cast (926) is said to be louder than that of rocks hurled from a large siege-engine, louder than thunder (921–3); the spear flies 'with the force of a dark whirlwind' (923); when it hits Turnus, groans from the onlookers echo throughout the landscape (928–9). Aeneas' spear itself is 'huge', indeed 'like a tree' (888); the rock that Turnus picks up is likewise 'huge' (896–7): Virgil says it could only be lifted by twelve men nowadays (899–900). This aspect of Virgil's style is not to everyone's taste; but it is a key part of his account of the single combat, and certainly raises the intensity of that narrative.

Virgil has always been admired for the sound of his poetry (even by those who do not think much of its content). This is partly a product of his metrical skill (see below); but he is also a master of choosing and arranging words so that the sounds they make serve either to emphasize or to illustrate what they mean.

This can involve the use of alliteration. Thus, for example, Aeneas' final words in the poem gain intensity through (among other means) repeated 'p' and 's' sounds:

'Pallas te hoc vulnere, Pallas
immolat et poenam scelerato ex sanguine sumit.'

(948–9)

Or, when Turnus' sword breaks during the first part of the single combat, the alliteration of brittle 'c', 's' and 't' sounds is onomatopoeic:

mortalis mucro glacies ceu futtilis ictu
dissiluit . . .

(740–1)

The profusion of vowel sounds in Latin allows Virgil to make even more extensive use of assonance, to similar ends. For instance, when Turnus is hit by Aeneas' spear, the Rutulians' groans and their echo in the landscape are audible in the 'u' sounds:

consurgunt gemitu Rutuli totusque remugit
mons circum . . .

(928–9)

Similar onomatopoeia is found in the final line of the poem, as Turnus' life departs with a groan:

vitaque cum gemitu fugit indignata sub umbras.

(952)

Examples such as these could be multiplied many times. It is worth remembering as you read Virgil that the Romans would very often encounter literature read aloud – either read by others, or read aloud by readers to themselves. Try doing the same thing yourself and see what you can hear.

Virgil's language: Some challenges

Virgil's Latin is at times not straightforward even for scholars; for the student coming straight from GCSE, or after a year of A Level, it presents multiple challenges. We shall here briefly consider some of the most significant of these.

The most obvious challenge is one of vocabulary. Virgil, like most poets, has a rich vocabulary; naturally, the range of words in *Aeneid* XII is far wider than the 850 or so on the AS Latin vocabulary list. Even those words which are on the AS list may have meanings in the *Aeneid* which are not found on that list. The Vocabulary at the back of this book contains all the words used in the AS Level and A Level set texts. When considering the meanings these words have in *Aeneid* XII, I have made much use of the *OLD* (*Oxford Latin Dictionary*) and sometimes cite that work in the commentary; it is the most helpful and reliable resource in English for seeing the range of possible nuances of any given Latin word.

Once one knows what the individual words in a Latin sentence mean, one then has to work out the meaning of the whole. In the *Aeneid*, probably the biggest challenge in this respect is presented by word order, which is generally far more free in verse than it is in prose. Words do not necessarily appear where one expects them: for example, verbs are frequently not at the end of a clause, and nouns and adjectives which agree with each other are often not adjacent (this separation of noun from adjective is known as 'hyperbaton'). A first encounter with

Latin verse can be intimidating for this reason; the best advice is to try to keep one's head, and aim to apply the normal approach as far as possible: that is, find the verb, then the subject and object if they are present, then try to see how the rest of the words relate to these. One thing about the *Aeneid* which is helpful in this respect is that Virgil's sentence structure tends not to be too complex: subordinate clauses are much less frequent than in many Latin prose authors.

Complexity of case usage is one of the most challenging features of original Latin texts. The A Level language syllabus encourages one to move beyond the vital but simple rules learned at GCSE (with genitive meaning 'of', dative 'to' or 'for', and ablative 'by', 'with' or 'from'); but even so, the range of usages found in Virgil will include some for which little preparation will have been likely. The commentary aims to help with these (it should be noted that identifications of some usages are provisional, rather than definitive: it is not always clear exactly what function a case serves in a clause). One general point worth noting at the outset is that poetry is much more free than prose in omitting prepositions and allowing the case endings of nouns to do the prepositions' work; so, for instance, 'in (a place)' is often expressed by an ablative without the preposition *in*.

Omission of words ('ellipsis') is, indeed, a feature of Latin style which occurs more generally, and to which it takes time to adjust. Authors of both verse and prose regularly leave out words which they think can easily be supplied or understood by a reader who is paying attention. Those most commonly left out are parts of the verb 'to be', and nouns or pronouns for adjectives or participles which are included. But often the ellipsis will be less straightforward, and elements will need to be supplied from another phrase, clause or sentence nearby: this is sometimes called the *apo koinou* construction (32–3n.), and it is found many times in *Aeneid* XII.

Three pervasive characteristics of the narrative style of the *Aeneid* might initially confuse. First, Virgil very frequently uses present-tense verbs to narrate events which took place in the past (see XII.1–4 for examples). Indeed, this 'historic present' is found more often in the *Aeneid* than past tense verbs. Such present tenses should be translated as past in English. Second, adjectives regularly do the duty of adverbs; translation should reflect this (at XII.3, for instance, *implacabilis ardet* means 'he burned implacably'). Third, plural nouns are often used to denote things which are singular (for example, *ora* at XII.66 or 82), and occasionally a singular noun denotes something plural (XII.750 genitive *pennae*).

The commentary contains notes explaining other stylistic features which may be unfamiliar and potentially confusing: for example, metonymy (1n.), hendiadys (41–2n.), litotes (50n.), tmesis (61n.), *pars pro toto* (88–9n.), prolepsis (94n.), 'theme and variation' (617–19n.), the *figura etymologica* (638n.), adversative asyndeton (663–4n.), the 'transferred epithet' (859n.), *hysteron proteron* (924–5n.) and zeugma (930–1n.).

Lastly, Virgil makes use of a number of variant verb forms which are not found on the A Level language syllabus. Look out for third-person plural perfect active forms ending in *-ere* rather than *-erunt* (12n.), for 'syncopated' forms of perfect active verbs (633n.) and for second-person singular present passive subjunctive forms ending in *-are* rather than *-aris* (33n.).

Metre

Classical poetry is written in so-called 'quantitative' metres, in which rhythm is created by patterns of long and short syllables. 'Quantity' is the technical term for the length of a syllable.

The *Aeneid*, like most surviving Greek and Latin epic poetry, is written in the hexameter metre. The pattern of syllables for the hexameter is as follows (with long syllables marked – and short syllables ∪):

1	2	3	4	5	6
$-\cup\cup$	$\mid-\cup\cup$	$\mid-\cup\cup$	$\mid-\cup\cup$	$\mid-\cup\cup$	$\mid-\cup$
$--$	$\mid--$	$\mid--$	$\mid--$	$\mid--$	$\mid--$

Every complete hexameter line is made up of six *metra* or metrical 'feet'. Each foot contains either two or three syllables. In every foot in the hexameter, the first syllable must be long; it is followed either by one long syllable or by two short syllables – except in the case of the sixth foot, where it is followed either by one long syllable or by one short syllable. Thus, each of the first five feet in a hexameter will be either a 'dactyl' (as the pattern – ∪ ∪ is known) or a 'spondee' (– –); the sixth foot will either be a 'trochee' (– ∪) or a 'spondee' (– –).

Hexameter lines can therefore vary quite widely, both in the number of syllables they contain (from 12 to 17) and in the type of feet which make up the line. This potential for variety is one of the attractions of the hexameter for epic poets, whose poems contain very many lines: the variation in the rhythm from line to line avoids monotony.

'Scansion' is the technical term for the identification of the precise rhythm of a metrical line of poetry. Scansion of a hexameter requires the reader to establish the 'quantities' of the various syllables in the line – to establish, that is, which syllables are short and which long.

Every syllable in a Latin word contains a vowel sound; this sound will have a natural pronunciation as either short (like the first 'a' of *amamus*) or long (like the second 'a' of *amamus*). (Note that double vowels – so-called 'diphthongs', like *-ae-* – are pronounced as one long syllable.) Often this natural pronunciation of a word will determine whether a syllable in a hexameter is to be considered short or long. But the situation is more complex than this.

One factor complicating scansion is the rule that vowel sounds which are naturally short are lengthened (that is, they are considered and pronounced as long) if they are followed by an 'x', by a 'z' or by two or more consonants (unless the second of those consonants is an 'l' or an 'r', in which case the vowel can either remain short or be lengthened). This 'lengthening by position' will take place even if the two consonants following the vowel are not in the same word as that vowel.

(Note that the combination *qu* is considered a single consonant for the purposes of scansion, and that the letter 'i' sometimes functions as a consonant rather than a vowel – for example, in the word *iam*, which has one syllable rather than two.)

Scansion is also complicated by the phenomenon known as 'elision'. If a vowel or diphthong (or a vowel followed by the letter 'm') at the end of a word is followed by a word beginning with a vowel, a diphthong or an 'h', the final syllable of the first word is typically 'elided': that is, it is pronounced so lightly that it virtually disappears, and it is ignored in scansion. (Very occasionally, elision of such a syllable does not take place; such neglect of elision is known as 'hiatus': instances can be found in the set texts at, e.g., XII.31, 648).

Two further points should be observed. First, the fifth foot of the hexameter is almost always a 'dactyl' (– ∪ ∪); of the 952 lines in *Aeneid* XII, for instance, only two (12.83, 863) contain 'spondees' (– –) in the fifth foot. Second, hexameter lines typically feature a word-break (one word ends and another begins) in the middle of the third foot – usually after the first long syllable of either a dactyl or a spondee, but sometimes after the first short syllable of a dactyl. If there is no word-break in the third foot, there must be one in the fourth foot (which is often accompanied by another in the second foot). These word-breaks are known as 'caesuras'; it is conventional for them to be marked when the scansion of a hexameter line is written out.

To give you an idea of how some of the various rules we have mentioned work in practice, the first four lines of *Aeneid* XII are scanned as follows:

    – ∪ ∪| – – |–/–| – – | – ∪∪| – –
    Turnus ut infractos adverso Marte Latinos

‒‒|‒ ∪ ∪|‒/ ∪∪| ‒   ‒ | ‒ ∪ ∪| ‒ ‒
defecisse videt, sua nunc promissa reposci,

‒ ‒ | ‒   ∪ ∪|‒/‒| ‒   ‒|‒∪∪|‒ ∪
se signar(i) oculis, ultr(o) implacabilis ardet

‒ ‒ |‒   ∪∪| ‒ / ‒ |‒ ‒ | ‒ ∪ ∪ |‒ ‒
attollitqu(e) animos. Poenorum qualis in arvis

The text of this edition

The Latin text used in this edition is based on that of the Oxford Classical Text edited by Sir Roger Mynors (Oxford, 1972: corrected edition), the most widely used modern edition of Virgil. At 12.714 I have preferred *miscentur* to *miscetur*, and there are occasional departures from Mynors' punctuation (at 12.6, 30, 48, 57, 59, 76, 102, 628, 662, 664, 676, 678, 830, 838, 847, 915, 934 and 937). Otherwise, the only changes are the conversion of accusative plurals ending in –*is* to –*es*, and of consonantal 'u' to 'v'.

Further reading

Various English translations of the *Aeneid* exist. The most reliable modern guide to the meaning of the Latin is probably David West's (Harmondsworth, 1990); to my mind the most appealing version for sustained reading is that of Robert Fitzgerald (London, 1984). There is an outstanding translation of the *Georgics* by L. P. Wilkinson (Harmondsworth, 1982); for the *Eclogues*, try the version of Guy Lee (Harmondsworth, 1984).

A number of commentaries on *Aeneid* XII exist. The finest, fullest and most recent edition is Richard Tarrant's (Cambridge, 2012); this is

particularly strong on literary interpretation. The shorter editions of
W. S. Maguinness (London, 1953) and B. Tilly (London, 1969) are
useful. A. Traina's *Virgilio. L'utopia e la storia* (Turin, 1997; Italian) is
very helpful on the language of *Aeneid* XII.

P. Hardie, *Virgil* (Oxford, 1998) and J. Griffin, *Virgil* (Oxford, 1986)
are good general books on Virgil. On the poet's life and career:
N. Horsfall, *A Companion to the Study of Virgil* (Leiden, 1995),
pp. 1–25. For the historical background: R. Syme, *The Roman
Revolution* (Oxford, 1939); A. Wallace-Hadrill, *Augustan Rome*
(London, 2018, 2nd edn). Shakespeare's *Julius Caesar* and *Antony and
Cleopatra* offer an attractive 'way in' to the high politics of the period.

The finest modern book on the *Aeneid* is R. Heinze, *Virgil's Epic
Technique* (Bristol, 1993; the German original was published in 1903).
V. Pöschl, *The Art of Virgil: Image and Symbol in the Aeneid* (Michigan,
1962) is highly recommended. W. A. Camps, *An Introduction to Virgil's
Aeneid* (Oxford, 1969) lives up to its title. Chapter 4 of D. Feeney's *The
Gods in Epic* (Oxford, 1991) considers the *Aeneid*. S. J. Harrison (ed.),
Oxford Readings in Virgil's Aeneid (Oxford, 1990) gathers many
excellent pieces: among them, G. Knauer, 'Virgil's *Aeneid* and Homer',
and W. S. Anderson, 'Virgil's Second *Iliad*', discuss the relationship
between the *Aeneid* and Homer. F. Mac Góráin and C. Martindale
(eds), *The Cambridge Companion to Virgil* (Cambridge, 2019, 2nd
edn) contains stimulating essays on a range of topics.

On the interpretation of the final scene of the poem, see the
introduction to Tarrant's edition, pp. 16–30, and N. Horsfall, *A
Companion to the Study of Virgil* (Leiden, 1995), pp. 192–216.

Maguinness' edition of *Aeneid* XII has an excellent section on
metre (pp. 20–36). More generally on this topic, see S. E. Winbolt,
Latin Hexameter Verse (London, 1903).

Text

Turnus ut infractos adverso Marte Latinos
defecisse videt, sua nunc promissa reposci,
se signari oculis, ultro implacabilis ardet
attollitque animos. Poenorum qualis in arvis
saucius ille gravi venantum vulnere pectus   5
tum demum movet arma leo gaudetque comantes
excutiens cervice toros fixumque latronis
impavidus frangit telum et fremit ore cruento:
haud secus accenso gliscit violentia Turno.
tum sic adfatur regem atque ita turbidus infit: 10
'nulla mora in Turno; nihil est quod dicta retractent
ignavi Aeneadae, nec quae pepigere recusent:
congredior. fer sacra, pater, et concipe foedus.
aut hac Dardanium dextra sub Tartara mittam
desertorem Asiae (sedeant spectentque Latini),   15
et solus ferro crimen commune refellam,
aut habeat victos, cedat Lavinia coniunx.'
olli sedato respondit corde Latinus:
'o praestans animi iuvens, quantum ipse feroci
virtute exsuperas, tanto me impensius aequum est   20
consulere atque omnes metuentem expendere casus.
sunt tibi regna patris Dauni, sunt oppida capta
multa manu, nec non aurumque animusque Latino est;
sunt aliae innuptae Latio et Laurentibus arvis
nec genus indecores. sine me haec haud mollia fatu   25
sublatis aperire dolis, simul hoc animo hauri:
me natam nulli veterum sociare procorum
fas erat, idque omnes divique hominesque canebant.
victus amore tui, cognato sanguine victus
coniugis et maestae lacrimis, vincla omnia rupi: 30
promissam eripui genero, arma impia sumpsi.

ex illo qui me casus, quae, Turne, sequantur
bella, vides, quantos primus patiare labores.
bis magna victi pugna vix urbe tuemur
spes Italas; recalent nostro Thybrina fluenta   35
sanguine adhuc campique ingentes ossibus albent.
quo referor totiens? quae mentem insania mutat?
si Turno exstincto socios sum ascire paratus,
cur non incolumi potius certamina tollo?
quid consanguinei Rutuli, quid cetera dicet   40
Italia, ad mortem si te (fors dicta refutet!)
prodiderim, natam et conubia nostra petentem?
respice res bello varias, miserere parentis
longaevi, quem nunc maestum patria Ardea longe
dividit.' haudquaquam dictis violentia Turni   45
flectitur; exsuperat magis aegrescitque medendo.
ut primum fari potuit, sic institit ore:
'quam pro me curam geris, hanc, precor, optime, pro me
deponas letumque sinas pro laude pacisci.
et nos tela, pater, ferrumque haud debile dextra   50
spargimus, et nostro sequitur de vulnere sanguis.
longe illi dea mater erit, quae nube fugacem
feminea tegat et vanis sese occulat umbris.'
at regina nova pugnae conterrita sorte
flebat et ardentem generum moritura tenebat: 55
'Turne, per has ego te lacrimas, per si quis Amatae
tangit honos animum – spes tu nunc una, senectae
tu requies miserae, decus imperiumque Latini
te penes, in te omnis domus inclinata recumbit –
unum oro: desiste manum committere Teucris.   60
qui te cumque manent isto certamine casus
et me, Turne, manent; simul haec invisa relinquam
lumina nec generum Aenean captiva videbo.'
accepit vocem lacrimis Lavinia matris
flagrantes perfusa genas, cui plurimus ignem   65
subiecit rubor et calefacta per ora cucurrit.

Indum sanguineo veluti violaverit ostro
si quis ebur, aut mixta rubent ubi lilia multa
alba rosa, tales virgo dabat ore colores.

illum turbat amor figitque in virgine vultus;   70
ardet in arma magis paucisque adfatur Amatam:
'ne, quaeso, ne me lacrimis neve omine tanto
prosequere in duri certamina Martis euntem,
o mater; neque enim Turno mora libera mortis.

nuntius haec, Idmon, Phrygio mea dicta tyranno   75
haud placitura refer: cum primum crastina caelo
puniceis invecta rotis Aurora rubebit,
non Teucros agat in Rutulos, Teucrum arma quiescant
et Rutuli; nostro dirimamus sanguine bellum,
illo quaeratur coniunx Lavinia campo.'   80

haec ubi dicta dedit rapidusque in tecta recessit,
poscit equos gaudetque tuens ante ora frementes,
Pilumno quos ipsa decus dedit Orithyia,
qui candore nives anteirent, cursibus auras.

circumstant properi aurigae manibusque lacessunt   85
pectora plausa cavis et colla comantia pectunt.

ipse dehinc auro squalentem alboque orichalco
circumdat loricam umeris, simul aptat habendo
ensemque clipeumque et rubrae cornua cristae,
ensem quem Dauno ignipotens deus ipse parenti   90
fecerat et Stygia candentem tinxerat unda.

exim quae mediis ingenti adnixa columnae
aedibus astabat, validam vi corripit hastam,
Actoris Aurunci spolium, quassatque trementem
vociferans: 'nunc, o numquam frustrata vocatus   95
hasta meos, nunc tempus adest: te maximus Actor,
te Turni nunc dextra gerit; da sternere corpus
loricamque manu valida lacerare revulsam
semiviri Phrygis et foedare in pulvere crines
vibratos calido ferro murraque madentes.'   100
his agitur furiis, totoque ardentis ab ore

scintillae absistunt, oculis micat acribus ignis:
mugitus veluti cum prima in proelia taurus
terrificos ciet aut irasci in cornua temptat
arboris obnixus trunco, ventosque lacessit   105
ictibus aut sparsa ad pugnam proludit harena.

*107–613: Aeneas is keen to fight, and the next morning preparations are
made for the single combat; but the goddess Juno intervenes to disrupt
these, and battle between the Trojans and Italians recommences. Aeneas
is wounded, but after being healed he returns to the field and soon
begins an assault on Latinus' city. The citizens panic, and Queen Amata
kills herself in despair.*

interea extremo bellator in aequore Turnus
palantes sequitur paucos iam segnior atque   615
iam minus atque minus successu laetus equorum.
attulit hunc illi caecis terroribus aura
commixtum clamorem, arrectasque impulit aures
confusae sonus urbis et inlaetabile murmur.
'ei mihi! quid tanto turbantur moenia luctu?   620
quisve ruit tantus diversa clamor ab urbe?'
sic ait, adductisque amens subsistit habenis.
atque huic, in faciem soror ut conversa Metisci
aurigae currumque et equos et lora regebat,
talibus occurrit dictis: 'hac, Turne, sequamur   625
Troiugenas, qua prima viam victoria pandit;
sunt alii qui tecta manu defendere possint.
ingruit Aeneas Italis et proelia miscet:
et nos saeva manu mittamus funera Teucris.
nec numero inferior pugnae neque honore recedes.'   630
Turnus ad haec:
'o soror, et dudum agnovi, cum prima per artem
foedera turbasti teque haec in bella dedisti,
et nunc nequiquam fallis dea. sed quis Olympo

demissam tantos voluit te ferre labores?   635
an fratris miseri letum ut crudele videres?
nam quid ago? aut quae iam spondet Fortuna salutem?
vidi oculos ante ipse meos me voce vocantem
Murranum, quo non superat mihi carior alter,
oppetere ingentem atque ingenti vulnere victum.   640
occidit infelix ne nostrum dedecus Ufens
aspiceret; Teucri potiuntur corpore et armis.
exscindine domos (id rebus defuit unum)
perpetiar, dextra nec Drancis dicta refellam?
terga dabo et Turnum fugientem haec terra videbit?   645
usque adeone mori miserum est? vos o mihi, Manes,
este boni, quoniam superis aversa voluntas.
sancta ad vos anima atque istius inscia culpae
descendam magnorum haud umquam indignus avorum.'
vix ea fatus erat: medios volat ecce per hostes   650
vectus equo spumante Saces, adversa sagitta
saucius ora, ruitque implorans nomine Turnum:
'Turne, in te suprema salus, miserere tuorum.
fulminat Aeneas armis summasque minatur
deiecturum arces Italum excidioque daturum,   655
iamque faces ad tecta volant. in te ora Latini,
in te oculos referunt; mussat rex ipse Latinus
quos generos vocet aut quae sese ad foedera flectat.
praeterea regina, tui fidissima, dextra
occidit ipsa sua lucemque exterrita fugit.   660
soli pro portis Messapus et acer Atinas
sustentant acies; circum hos utrimque phalanges
stant densae strictisque seges mucronibus horret
ferrea. tu currum deserto in gramine versas.'
obstipuit varia confusus imagine rerum   665
Turnus et obtutu tacito stetit; aestuat ingens
uno in corde pudor mixtoque insania luctu
et furiis agitatus amor et conscia virtus.
ut primum discussae umbrae et lux reddita menti,

ardentes oculorum orbes ad moenia torsit 670
turbidus eque rotis magnam respexit ad urbem.
ecce autem flammis inter tabulata volutus
ad caelum undabat vertex turrimque tenebat,
turrim compactis trabibus quam eduxerat ipse
subdideratque rotas pontesque instraverat altos. 675
'iam iam fata, soror, superant: absiste morari;
quo deus et quo dura vocat Fortuna sequamur.
stat conferre manum Aeneae, stat quidquid acerbi est
morte pati, neque me indecorem, germana, videbis
amplius. hunc, oro, sine me furere ante furorem.' 680
dixit, et e curru saltum dedit ocius arvis
perque hostes, per tela ruit maestamque sororem
deserit ac rapido cursu media agmina rumpit.
ac veluti montis saxum de vertice praeceps
cum ruit avulsum vento, seu turbidus imber 685
proluit aut annis solvit sublapsa vetustas;
fertur in abruptum magno mons improbus actu
exsultatque solo, silvas armenta virosque
involvens secum: disiecta per agmina Turnus
sic urbis ruit ad muros, ubi plurima fuso 690
sanguine terra madet striduntque hastilibus aurae,
significatque manu et magno simul incipit ore:
'parcite iam, Rutuli, et vos tela inhibete, Latini.
quaecumque est fortuna, mea est; me verius unum
pro vobis foedus luere et decernere ferro.' 695
discessere omnes medii spatiumque dedere.
at pater Aeneas audito nomine Turni
deserit et muros et summas deserit arces
praecipitatque moras omnes, opera omnia rumpit
laetitia exsultans horrendumque intonat armis: 700
quantus Athos aut quantus Eryx aut ipse coruscis
cum fremit ilicibus quantus gaudetque nivali
vertice se attollens pater Appenninus ad auras.
iam vero et Rutuli certatim et Troes et omnes

convertere oculos Itali, quique alta tenebant   705
moenia quique imos pulsabant ariete muros,
armaque deposuere umeris. stupet ipse Latinus
ingentes, genitos diversis partibus orbis,
inter se coiisse viros et cernere ferro.
atque illi, ut vacuo patuerunt aequore campi,   710
procursu rapido coniectis eminus hastis
invadunt Martem clipeis atque aere sonoro.
dat gemitum tellus; tum crebros ensibus ictus
congeminant, fors et virtus miscentur in unum.
ac velut ingenti Sila summove Taburno   715
cum duo conversis inimica in proelia tauri
frontibus incurrunt, pavidi cessere magistri,
stat pecus omne metu mutum, mussantque iuvencae
quis nemori imperitet, quem tota armenta sequantur;
illi inter sese multa vi vulnera miscent   720
cornuaque obnixi infigunt et sanguine largo
colla armosque lavant, gemitu nemus omne remugit:
non aliter Tros Aeneas et Daunius heros
concurrunt clipeis, ingens fragor aethera complet.
Iuppiter ipse duas aequato examine lances   725
sustinet et fata imponit diversa duorum,
quem damnet labor et quo vergat pondere letum.

emicat hic impune putans et corpore toto
alte sublatum consurgit Turnus in ensem
et ferit; exclamant Troes trepidique Latini, 730
arrectaeque amborum acies. at perfidus ensis
frangitur in medioque ardentem deserit ictu,
ni fuga subsidio subeat. fugit ocior Euro
ut capulum ignotum dextramque aspexit inermem.
fama est praecipitem, cum prima in proelia iunctos 735
conscendebat equos, patrio mucrone relicto,
dum trepidat, ferrum aurigae rapuisse Metisci;
idque diu, dum terga dabant palantia Teucri,
suffecit; postquam arma dei ad Volcania ventum est,
mortalis mucro glacies ceu futtilis ictu 740
dissiluit, fulva resplendent fragmina harena.
ergo amens diversa fuga petit aequora Turnus
et nunc huc, inde huc incertos implicat orbes;
undique enim densa Teucri inclusere corona
atque hinc vasta palus, hinc ardua moenia cingunt. 745
nec minus Aeneas, quamquam tardata sagitta
interdum genua impediunt cursumque recusant,
insequitur trepidique pedem pede fervidus urget:
inclusum veluti si quando flumine nactus
cervum aut puniceae saeptum formidine pennae 750
venator cursu canis et latratibus instat;
ille autem insidiis et ripa territus alta
mille fugit refugitque vias, at vividus Umber
haeret hians, iam iamque tenet similisque tenenti
increpuit malis morsuque elusus inani est; 755
tum vero exoritur clamor ripaeque lacusque
responsant circa et caelum tonat omne tumultu.
ille simul fugiens Rutulos simul increpat omnes
nomine quemque vocans notumque efflagitat ensem.
Aeneas mortem contra praesensque minatur 760
exitium, si quisquam adeat, terretque trementes
excisurum urbem minitans et saucius instat.

quinque orbes explent cursu totidemque retexunt
huc illuc; neque enim levia aut ludicra petuntur
praemia, sed Turni de vita et sanguine certant.   765
forte sacer Fauno foliis oleaster amaris
hic steterat, nautis olim venerabile lignum,
servati ex undis ubi figere dona solebant
Laurenti divo et votas suspendere vestes;
sed stirpem Teucri nullo discrimine sacrum   770
sustulerant, puro ut possent concurrere campo.
hic hasta Aeneae stabat, huc impetus illam
detulerat fixam et lenta radice tenebat.
incubuit voluitque manu convellere ferrum
Dardanides, teloque sequi quem prendere cursu   775
non poterat. tum vero amens formidine Turnus
'Faune, precor, miserere' inquit 'tuque optima ferrum
Terra tene, colui vestros si semper honores,
quos contra Aeneadae bello fecere profanos.'
dixit, opemque dei non cassa in vota vocavit.   780
namque diu luctans lentoque in stirpe moratus
viribus haud ullis valuit discludere morsus
roboris Aeneas. dum nititur acer et instat,
rursus in aurigae faciem mutata Metisci
procurrit fratrique ensem dea Daunia reddit.   785
quod Venus audaci nymphae indignata licere
accessit telumque alta ab radice revellit.
olli sublimes armis animisque refecti,
hic gladio fidens, hic acer et arduus hasta,
adsistunt contra certamina Martis anheli.   790
Iunonem interea rex omnipotentis Olympi
adloquitur fulva pugnas de nube tuentem:
'quae iam finis erit, coniunx? quid denique restat?
indigetem Aenean scis ipsa et scire fateris
deberi caelo fatisque ad sidera tolli.   795
quid struis? aut qua spe gelidis in nubibus haeres?
mortalin decuit violari vulnere divum?'

aut ensem (quid enim sine te Iuturna valeret?)
ereptum reddi Turno et vim crescere victis?
desine iam tandem precibusque inflectere nostris,   800
ne te tantus edit tacitam dolor et mihi curae
saepe tuo dulci tristes ex ore recursent.
ventum ad supremum est. terris agitare vel undis
Troianos potuisti, infandum accendere bellum,
deformare domum et luctu miscere hymenaeos: 805
ulterius temptare veto.' sic Iuppiter orsus;
sic dea summisso contra Saturnia vultu:
'ista quidem quia nota mihi tua, magne, voluntas,
Iuppiter, et Turnum et terras invita reliqui;
nec tu me aeria solam nunc sede videres   810
digna indigna pati, sed flammis cincta sub ipsa
starem acie traheremque inimica in proelia Teucros.
Iuturnam misero (fateor) succurrere fratri
suasi et pro vita maiora audere probavi,
non ut tela tamen, non ut contenderet arcum;   815
adiuro Stygii caput implacabile fontis,
una superstitio superis quae reddita divis.
et nunc cedo equidem pugnasque exosa relinquo.
illud te, nulla fati quod lege tenetur,
pro Latio obtestor, pro maiestate tuorum: 820
cum iam conubiis pacem felicibus (esto)
component, cum iam leges et foedera iungent,
ne vetus indigenas nomen mutare Latinos
neu Troas fieri iubeas Teucrosque vocari
aut vocem mutare viros aut vertere vestem.   825
sit Latium, sint Albani per saecula reges,
sit Romana potens Itala virtute propago:
occidit, occideritque sinas cum nomine Troia.'
olli subridens hominum rerumque repertor:
'es germana Iovis Saturnique altera proles: 830
irarum tantos volvis sub pectore fluctus.
verum age et inceptum frustra summitte furorem:

do quod vis, et me victusque volensque remitto.
sermonem Ausonii patrium moresque tenebunt,
utque est nomen erit; commixti corpore tantum   835
subsident Teucri. morem ritusque sacrorum
adiciam faciamque omnes uno ore Latinos.
hinc genus Ausonio mixtum quod sanguine surget
supra homines, supra ire deos pietate videbis,
nec gens ulla tuos aeque celebrabit honores.'   840
adnuit his Iuno et mentem laetata retorsit;
interea excedit caelo nubemque relinquit.
his actis aliud genitor secum ipse volutat
Iuturnamque parat fratris dimittere ab armis.
dicuntur geminae pestes cognomine Dirae,   845
quas et Tartaream Nox intempesta Megaeram
uno eodemque tulit partu paribusque revinxit
serpentum spiris ventosasque addidit alas.
hae Iovis ad solium saevique in limine regis
apparent acuuntque metum mortalibus aegris,   850
si quando letum horrificum morbosque deum rex
molitur, meritas aut bello territat urbes.
harum unam celerem demisit ab aethere summo
Iuppiter inque omen Iuturnae occurrere iussit:
illa volat celerique ad terram turbine fertur.   855
non secus ac nervo per nubem impulsa sagitta,
armatam saevi Parthus quam felle veneni,
Parthus sive Cydon, telum immedicabile, torsit,
stridens et celeres incognita transilit umbras:
talis se sata Nocte tulit terrasque petivit.   860
postquam acies videt Iliacas atque agmina Turni,
alitis in parvae subitam collecta figuram,
quae quondam in bustis aut culminibus desertis
nocte sedens serum canit importuna per umbras –
hanc versa in faciem Turni se pestis ob ora   865
fertque refertque sonans clipeumque everberat alis.
illi membra novus solvit formidine torpor,

A
Level

arrectaeque horrore comae et vox faucibus haesit.
at procul ut Dirae stridorem agnovit et alas,
infelix crines scindit Iuturna solutos   870
unguibus ora soror foedans et pectora pugnis:
'quid nunc te tua, Turne, potest germana iuvare?
aut quid iam durae superat mihi? qua tibi lucem
arte morer? talin possum me opponere monstro?
iam iam linquo acies. ne me terrete timentem,   875
obscenae volucres: alarum verbera nosco
letalemque sonum, nec fallunt iussa superba
magnanimi Iovis. haec pro virginitate reponit?
quo vitam dedit aeternam? cur mortis adempta est
condicio? possem tantos finire dolores   880
nunc certe, et misero fratri comes ire per umbras!
immortalis ego? aut quicquam mihi dulce meorum
te sine, frater, erit? o quae satis ima dehiscat
terra mihi, Manesque deam demittat ad imos?'
tantum effata caput glauco contexit amictu   885
multa gemens et se fluvio dea condidit alto.
Aeneas instat contra telumque coruscat
ingens arboreum, et saevo sic pectore fatur:
'quae nunc deinde mora est? aut quid iam, Turne, retractas?
non cursu, saevis certandum est comminus armis.   890
verte omnes tete in facies et contrahe quidquid
sive animis sive arte vales; opta ardua pennis
astra sequi clausumque cava te condere terra.'
ille caput quassans: 'non me tua fervida terrent
dicta, ferox; di me terrent et Iuppiter hostis.'   895
nec plura effatus saxum circumspicit ingens,
saxum antiquum ingens, campo quod forte iacebat,
limes agro positus litem ut discerneret arvis.
vix illum lecti bis sex cervice subirent,
qualia nunc hominum producit corpora tellus;   900
ille manu raptum trepida torquebat in hostem
altior insurgens et cursu concitus heros.

sed neque currentem se nec cognoscit euntem
tollentemve manu saxumve immane moventem;
genua labant, gelidus concrevit frigore sanguis.   905
tum lapis ipse viri vacuum per inane volutus
nec spatium evasit totum neque pertulit ictum.
ac velut in somnis, oculos ubi languida pressit
nocte quies, nequiquam avidos extendere cursus
velle videmur et in mediis conatibus aegri   910
succidimus; non lingua valet, non corpore notae
sufficiunt vires nec vox aut verba sequuntur:
sic Turno, quacumque viam virtute petivit,
successum dea dira negat. tum pectore sensus
vertuntur varii: Rutulos aspectat et urbem   915
cunctaturque metu letumque instare tremescit,
nec quo se eripiat, nec qua vi tendat in hostem,
nec currus usquam videt aurigamve sororem.
cunctanti telum Aeneas fatale coruscat,
sortitus fortunam oculis, et corpore toto   920
eminus intorquet. murali concita numquam
tormento sic saxa fremunt nec fulmine tanti
dissultant crepitus. volat atri turbinis instar
exitium dirum hasta ferens orasque recludit
loricae et clipei extremos septemplicis orbes;   925
per medium stridens transit femur. incidit ictus
ingens ad terram duplicato poplite Turnus.
consurgunt gemitu Rutuli totusque remugit
mons circum et vocem late nemora alta remittunt.
ille humilis supplex oculos dextramque precantem   930
protendens 'equidem merui nec deprecor' inquit;
'utere sorte tua. miseri te si qua parentis
tangere cura potest, oro (fuit et tibi talis
Anchises genitor), Dauni miserere senectae
et me, seu corpus spoliatum lumine mavis,   935
redde meis. vicisti et victum tendere palmas
Ausonii videre; tua est Lavinia coniunx:

**A
Level**

ulterius ne tende odiis.' stetit acer in armis
Aeneas volvens oculos dextramque repressit;
et iam iamque magis cunctantem flectere sermo   940
coeperat, infelix umero cum apparuit alto
balteus et notis fulserunt cingula bullis
Pallantis pueri, victum quem vulnere Turnus
straverat atque umeris inimicum insigne gerebat.
ille, oculis postquam saevi monimenta doloris   945
exuviasque hausit, furiis accensus et ira
terribilis: 'tune hinc spoliis indute meorum
eripiare mihi? Pallas te hoc vulnere, Pallas
immolat et poenam scelerato ex sanguine sumit.'
hoc dicens ferrum adverso sub pectore condit   950
fervidus; ast illi solvuntur frigore membra
vitaque cum gemitu fugit indignata sub umbras.

Commentary Notes

References to the *OLD* are to the *Oxford Latin Dictionary* (see p. 24).

For the narrative background to *Aeneid* XII, see pp. 8–10.

1–9

The opening lines of Book XII focus on Turnus and his response to the military reverse which his forces have just suffered.

1–4 We glimpse (through Turnus' eyes: **videt** 2) something of the impact of the defeat on the morale and behaviour of the soldiers.

1   adverso Marte: ablative either of cause or 'attendant circumstances', with **infractos** ('broken because the war was going badly' or 'broken, with the war going badly'). **Marte** is a metonymy (the use of the name of one thing to denote another thing with which it is associated): as Mars is the god of war, his name can be used to mean simply 'war', 'battle' or 'fighting'. **Latinos**: the 'men of Latium', who make up much of the army commanded by Turnus. Latium was the name of a district in central Italy, the borders of which were eventually the rivers Tiber and Liris to west and east, and the Mediterranean and the Apennine mountains to south and north.

1–2   Latinos/defecisse: accusative and infinitive following a verb of perceiving (**videt**), as are **sua ... promissa reposci** (2) and **se signari** (3).

2   videt: the verb is a historic present (as are **ardet** (3), **attollit** (4) and **gliscit** (9) later in this section); the use of the historic present in preference to past tense verbs is a pervasive feature of the *Aeneid* (see pp. 25–6). **sua ... promissa reposci: promissa** here refers, above all, to Turnus' promise to fight Aeneas in single combat (a promise made in public, at the council: XI.434–44); tr. '[when he saw] that redemption of his own promises was now being demanded'.

3   ultro: this word lacks a convenient equivalent in English, and must be translated according to the context in which it is found; it tends to describe action which goes beyond (this is the meaning of the related word *ultra*) what might be expected: thus, in this situation it would be understandable if Turnus were to share in the general dejection, but, in fact, 'without hesitation' (**ultro**) he 'burns implacably'. **implacabilis**: adjective used adverbially. **ardet**: p. 21.

4–8 Turnus is compared in an extended simile (pp. 20–1) to a lion wounded by hunters: the primary point of comparison (as line 9 makes clear) is the **violentia** surging in both beast and warrior when provoked, but, as often, there are further correspondences between simile and narrative.

4   Poenorum: extended similes often specify a particular location. Carthage was a city in North Africa; in antiquity, lions were found in North Africa.

5   saucius ... pectus: saucius is nominative agreeing with **leo** (6); **pectus** is accusative singular – an 'accusative of respect' after **saucius**, indicating where the lion is wounded. **gravi ... vulnere**: ablative of means after **saucius**, producing something of a tautology ('wounded by a serious wound'). **venantum**: masculine genitive plural of the present active participle of *venor* (deponent verbs are generally passive in form though active in meaning, but their present participles are active in form as well as meaning); the usual form in classical prose would be *venantium*, but poets often vary the *-ium* genitive plural ending to *-um*. The participle is here used as a substantive, and the genitive is subjective: tr. '[by a serious wound] from men hunting'.

AS

5–6   ille ... leo: the demonstrative adjective **ille** involves the reader in the simile, specifying a particular animal – as if the reader were present, watching.

6–7   gaudetque .../ excutiens: Virgil likes to use *gaudeo* with a participle (82, 702); elsewhere it usually governs an infinitive. **comantes/ excutiens cervice toros**: a *torus* on a body is usually a muscle (*OLD* 3), so this phrase literally means something like 'shaking out the muscles covered in hair on his neck'; but the expression can be understood as suggestive rather than literal: tr. 'shaking out the rippling mane on his neck'. **latronis**: one of the hunters (cf. **venantum** 5).

9   haud secus: **haud** is typically used to negative a single word. **violentia**: here, as often, denotes a violently passionate feeling (*OLD* 1b), rather than actions of physical violence (*OLD* 1a). **Turno**: dative of 'personal interest'; tr. 'the violent passion grew in Turnus' or 'the violent passion of Turnus grew'.

10–80

This scene takes place within Latinus' city (which is not named in the *Aeneid*). Precise details of the location are not given, but it is likely to be in or just outside the king's palace. By the end of the scene, five people seem to be present: the most important of these, Turnus and Latinus, are both explicitly there throughout the scene; Amata and Lavinia (54–5n.) – and Idmon (75n.) – should probably be understood as also present throughout, but by choosing not to indicate this until each character becomes involved, Virgil is able to generate some additional drama from the unexpectedness of their appearances.

10   sic adfatur ... atque ita ... infit: 'theme and variation' (617–19n.). **regem**: Latinus, the king of Latium.

AS

11-17   Turnus makes his intention and his determination immediately clear.

11   nulla mora in Turno: understand *est*. Turnus has a habit of referring to himself by his own name (cf. 74, 97, 645).

11-12   nihil est quod dicta retractent/ ignavi Aeneadae, nec quae pepigere recusent: tr. 'there is no reason why (*OLD nihil* 5) the cowardly followers of Aeneas should take back what has been said, and [there is] not [a reason why] they should refuse [those things] which they pledged'.

12   Aeneadae: this is the nominative plural form of the singular *Aeneades*; one form of Greek 'patronymic' (a word used to mean 'son of X') ends *-ides* (so, e.g., *Pelides* means 'son of Peleus') or *-ades*, and *Aeneades* thus literally means 'son of Aeneas': the plural form is used here and elsewhere in the *Aeneid* to mean 'followers of Aeneas'. **nec quae pepigere recusant**: understand *ea* ('those things') as the antecedent to **quae** (omission of *is/ea/id* as the antecedent to a relative clause is not uncommon); **pepigere** is an alternative form of *pepigerunt* (Latin poets often use this variant third-person plural perfect indicative ending in *-ere*, for reasons of metre or sound). Both **dicta** and **quae pepigere** in this sentence imply that Aeneas has pledged to fight Turnus in single combat: this is not quite true, although he had wished for such a duel at XI.116-18 and he will welcome the opportunity when it presents itself.

13   congredior: the present tense here expresses an immediate intention (cf. English 'I'm coming,' used by someone who has not quite set off). **sacra**: 'sacred things', as required for the solemn ratification of an agreement (**foedus** 13); at XII.119-20, fire and spring-water are specified. **pater**: use of this word often indicates a speaker's respect for the person addressed (*OLD* 5a); indeed, in Virgil, *pater* is used more commonly for this purpose than to acknowledge a blood relationship. Cf. 50, and *mater* addressed to Amata in 74.

14–15   Dardanium . . ./ desertorem Asiae: *Dardanius* is in origin a patronymic (12n.), meaning 'son of Dardanus' or 'descended from Dardanus' (which Aeneas literally is: Dardanus was grandfather of Tros, the founder of Troy and Aeneas' great-great-grandfather) – but on occasion in the *Aeneid*, it simply means 'Trojan'; either translation is valid here. **desertorem Asiae**: there were versions of the Trojan war myth in which Aeneas' departure was less than heroic, but Virgil's account in *Aeneid* II is very different; Turnus' allegation of cowardice has no validity in this poem.

14   hac . . . dextra: ablative of instrument, with **mittam; hac** refers to Turnus' own hand. **Tartara**: neuter accusative plural. Tartarus is the part of the underworld where the wicked are punished (cf. VI.548–627).

15   sedeant spectentque: jussive subjunctives.

16   ferro: ablative of instrument. The basic meaning of *ferrum* is 'iron'; it is also often used to mean 'a (specific) sword' (*OLD* 4), and sometimes – as here – 'the sword (as the instrument of fighting)' (*OLD* 5). **crimen commune refellam**: no 'accusation' has been voiced in the narrative, but Turnus presumably regards the Italians' flight from the Trojans and their allies in the battles of Books X and XI as something which might appear cowardly and disgraceful; he thinks that his confronting of Aeneas in single combat will be sufficient to dispel any such impression.

17   habeat victos: Aeneas is the unnamed subject; **habeat** is jussive subjunctive. **cedat Lavinia coniunx**: **cedat** is jussive subjunctive; **Lavinia** is the subject, **coniunx** is the predicate ('as [his] wife'). Lavinia, Latinus' daughter (cf. pp. 8–9), is seen as a prize in the war. She is probably present to hear these words (54–5n.); she is certainly present at 64–9 below.

18 olli: an archaic form of *illi* (dative singular of *ille*). **sedato . . . corde**: ablative of manner.

19–45 Latinus' reply is complex and impressive. With considerable tact (but also firmness on the key point: 27–31), he suggests that Turnus might withdraw his claim to Lavinia, and thus remove the need for further fighting – and the possibility of Turnus' own death.

19 o: the vocative particle **o** is usually reserved for emotional addresses (as here). **animi**: genitive of respect, in place of the more usual ablative after *praesto*. **iuvenis**: Turnus.

19–21 quantum ... tanto ... impensius ...: a comparative sentence with correlative adjectives.

19–20 quantum ipse feroci/ virtute exsuperas: quantum is accusative of extent (lit. 'as much as', but here tr. 'the more'); **feroci/ virtute** is ablative of respect after **exsuperas**; tr. 'the more you yourself excel in fierce-spirited bravery'.

20–1 tanto me impensius aequum est/ consulere atque omnes metuentem expendere casus: the construction is accusative (*me metuentem*) and infinitive (*consulere atque expendere*) after **aequum est**. **tanto** is ablative of measure of difference after the comparative adverb **impensius**: lit. 'by so much', but here tr. 'the more'; 'the more carefully it is right that I advise [you] and in my fear weigh up . . .'.

22 sunt tibi regna patris Dauni: tibi is possessive dative, 'there are belonging to you . . .'. Turnus' father Daunus does not appear in person in the *Aeneid*, but he is mentioned on a number of occasions (most of them in Book XII). He lives at Ardea (43–5); he is here portrayed as possessing a 'kingdom' (**regna** is presumably poetic plural) – a kingdom which is, indeed, expanding as a result of military successes (22–3).

AS

23   manu: 'by fighting', 'with arms' (*OLD* 9f); ablative of instrument with **capta. aurumque animusque Latino est: Latino** is possessive dative. **est** is singular despite a plurality of subjects. Repeated *-que* can sometimes mean 'both ... and ...'; but in epic the first *-que* is usually redundant, and need not be translated.

24   aliae innuptae: both adjectives; endings of Latin adjectives can suffice to indicate the persons to whom they refer: tr. 'other unmarried women'. **Latio et Laurentibus arvis:** ablatives of place where (without *in*: p. 25). **Laurentibus:** the 'Laurentine fields' are a coastal district of Latium (1n.); in the *Aeneid*, this is the area where Latinus' city is situated.

25   nec genus indecores: genus is accusative of respect.

25-6   Latinus prepares Turnus to hear his most important point, which will follow in lines 27–31 (to which **haec** 25 and **hoc** 26 refer).

25   sine: imperative of *sino*. **haud mollia fatu: fatu** is the ablative form of the supine of the verb *for*; tr. 'not easy to say'.

26   hoc: neuter accusative singular. **animo:** ablative of instrument, with **hauri;** tr. 'take this in with your mind'.

27-8   The prohibition to which Latinus here refers was conveyed to him by his father Faunus (VII.81–101). **me natam nulli veterum sociare procorum/ fas erat: fas** is followed by the accusative and infinitive *me sociare:* 'it was right for me to join'. **nulli** is dative singular; **veterum ... procorum** is partitive genitive: **veterum** here refers to suitors who are not 'old' in age, but 'old' in the sense that they were Lavinia's suitors previously (*OLD vetus* 2) – before Aeneas arrived. **omnes divique hominesque:** 23n.

29-31   Latinus here looks back to events narrated in *Aeneid* VII. The king initially welcomed the Trojans and betrothed Lavinia to

AS

Aeneas (VII.160–285); but through the agency of the goddess Juno, these arrangements were overturned (VII.286–640), not least by Amata (cf. XII.29–30) and Turnus (cf. XII.31), and the people of Latium took up arms against the Trojans (VII.620–817). In lines 29–31, it is notable that Latinus himself takes responsibility for events which, in fact, he tried to prevent (see VII.585–600, 616–19).

29–30 amore ... sanguine .../... lacrimis: all ablatives of means after **victus. tui**: objective genitive after **amore. cognato sanguine .../... coniugis et maestae lacrimis**: Latinus' wife Amata is related to Turnus; Virgil does not specify precisely how. Amata's tearful attempts to persuade Latinus to marry Lavinia to Turnus rather than to Aeneas are narrated at VII.358–72.

30 coniugis et maestae: the postponement of *et* from its expected position (here before *coniugis*) is a mannerism of Latin poetry from the first century BC onwards. **vincla**: here metaphorical, the word refers primarily to the 'bonds' restricting Latinus' freedom of action which resulted from the prohibition mentioned in lines 27–8; it may also refer to the moral/religious obligations he incurred once he had pledged his daughter to Aeneas and peace to the Trojans (the breaking of which pledges he emphasizes in line 31).

31 promissam eripui: understand *natam* (cf. 27); tr. 'I snatched [my daughter] away after she had been promised'. **genero**: dative of personal interest; the word refers to Aeneas – who was, in fact, not yet Latinus' son-in-law, but rather his 'prospective son-in-law' (*OLD gener* b); cf. 55.

32–3 vides is the main verb, here both literal ('you observe') and metaphorical ('you perceive (with your mind)'); it is followed by three indirect questions in asyndeton (**qui ... casus, quae .../ bella, quantos ... labores**). **ex illo: ex** is here either 'as a result of' or 'after'; **illo** is neuter, and refers back to the decisions (here seen as a single process) mentioned in 29–31. The phrase goes with all three indirect questions. **qui me casus**: the verb **sequantur**, which appears in the next indirect question (**quae . . . sequantur/ bella**) is to be understood in this clause also; this supplying of elements from one phrase, clause or sentence to another is known as the *apo koinou* construction. **casus . . ./ bella . . . labores**: Latinus here refers to the defeats in battle suffered in the previous two books of the *Aeneid*.

33 patiare: an alternative form of the second-person singular present passive subjunctive (the usual form is *patiaris*).

34 bis: first, that is, in the battle around the Trojan camp (narrated in Book X) and, second, on the plain before Latinus' city (in Book XI). **magna . . . pugna**: ablative of place where ('in a great battle'). **vix urbe tuemur/ spes Italas**: **urbe** is ablative of place where; **Italas**: 628n. After the battle in Book XI, the surviving cavalry retreated in disorder to Latinus' city – followed by Turnus and his infantry force; the city is now the one remaining stronghold of the Latin army and their allies.

35–6 recalent . . . albent: Latinus has just mentioned that all the Italians' hopes lay with the men in the city, after two defeats in battle; he now provides two clear visual indications of the scale of those defeats. **nostro . . ./ sanguine**: Latinus refers to losses among the Latins and their allies. **Thybrina fluenta**: the Tiber flows past the Trojan camp, which seems to be near the river's mouth; the area is the site of the limited fighting in Book IX, and of the full-scale battle in Book X.

37 quo referor totiens? In 29–36, Latinus has lamented his weakness in failing to confirm the arrangements which he made with the Trojans in Book VII; now he asks himself 'for what purpose do I slip backwards so many times?' **totiens** seems primarily to refer to the multiple errors mentioned in 29–31, although the present tense of **referor** shows that Latinus feels not only that he got things wrong in the past but also that his mistaken course has continued until now.

AS

quae mentem insania mutat? A development of *quo* in the previous question: having asked himself what purpose it has served to go back on his decisions in Book VII, the king now ponders whether some madness has possessed him (and still does: **mutat** is present) as he has continued in such courses of action.

38–45 After lamenting the weakness (37) that has led to disaster, Latinus now proposes decisive action. He believes that he can end the conflict (39). It is clear enough from the king's words that he thinks Turnus' withdrawal – from the fighting, and from the contest for Lavinia's hand – is an essential precondition for this arrangement; wisely and tactfully, however, the king does not state this point baldly: he prefers merely to imply it. Lines 38–9, 40–2 and 43–5 present three separate arguments in favour of his proposal; but since all three assume that should the conflict continue then defeat for Turnus is inevitable, it is not surprising that Turnus will go on to reject them (at 45–53).

38   socios ... ascire: socios refers to the Trojans, and the word is really a predicate here; tr. 'to admit [the Trojans as] allies'.

39   incolumi: understand **Turno** from 38 (*apo koinou*: 32–3n.), producing an ablative absolute parallel to **Turno exstincto** there. **cur non ... tollo?**: ordinarily, a deliberative question would feature a subjunctive verb; the indicative **tollo** may be colloquial, or may imply that the action mentioned here ('why am I not putting an end to the conflicts?') is less a floated possibility than something which Latinus is pretty certain he is going to carry out.

40–1   quid consanguinei Rutuli, quid cetera dicet/ Italia: *dicent* is to be understood with **quid consanguinei Rutuli** – the *apo koinou* construction again (32–3n.). **Rutuli**: the Rutulians were a historical people of southern Latium; their powerbase was the city of Ardea (44–5n.). In the *Aeneid*, they are ruled by Turnus' father Daunus (cf. 22n.) – hence **consanguinei** here – and Turnus leads their contingent within the Latin army (VII.783–802), as well as acting as field-commander for that whole army. **cetera . . ./ Italia**: 628n.

41–2 ad mortem si te . . ./ prodiderim: prodiderim is perfect subjunctive in a hypothetical condition; tr.'if I should abandon you to death'. **fors dicta refutet: refutet** is jussive subjunctive. Having mentioned the possibility of Turnus' death, Latinus inserts this wish in order to avert any bad omen which might come even from the words. **natam et conubia nostra petentem: petentem** agrees with **te** (41). **natam et conubia nostra** are probably best understood as a hendiadys – that is, the expression of a single idea by means of two phrases which are joined by 'and', rather than (as the reader expects) one modifying the other; tr. 'as you are seeking marriage with our daughter'.

43 miserere: second-person singular passive imperative, to be translated as active since *miseror* is deponent; the verb can take either an accusative or (as here: **parentis/ longaevi**) a genitive object.

43–4 parentis/longaevi: Daunus (22n.).

44–5 quem . . . patria Ardea longe/ dividit: 'whom his homeland keeps separate [from you], far off'. Ardea is in Latium, a little inland from the coast and about fifteen miles south of the mouth of the Tiber.

45–53 It is immediately clear that, for all his rhetorical skill and tact, Latinus has utterly failed to persuade Turnus. The young man's reply is passionate and proud; that said, it is also respectful and – considering the strength of his feelings – pretty controlled.

46 flectitur; exsuperat . . . aegrescit: the subject of all three verbs is **violentia**. The asyndeton between the sentence ending **flectitur** and that beginning **exsuperat** is 'adversative' (663–4n.). **aegrescitque medendo: medendo** is ablative of the gerund. Both words establish a medical image: Latinus' attempt to treat the patient has inadvertently made things worse.

47 ut primum fari potuit: Turnus' inability to speak before this point is presumably to be attributed to the force of his **violentia** (45–6). **institit ore**: *insisto* with *ore* (ablative of *os*) means 'I begin to speak out.'

48–9 The main verb is **precor**, which introduces an indirect command (here without *ut*); hence, the verbs **deponas** and **sinas** (both addressed to Latinus) are in the subjunctive mood. **quam pro me curam geris, hanc . . . pro me/ deponas**: the antecedent (**curam**) of the relative clause (**quam pro me . . . geris**) is drawn into the relative clause, as often; **hanc** makes it clear that **curam** is the object of **deponas** as well as **geris**. The two uses of **pro me** here differ slightly: the first means 'on my behalf', the second 'for my sake'.

49 letumque sinas pro laude pacisci: understand *me* as accusative object for **sinas**.

50–3 Turnus insists that if he is going to die (as he foresaw in line 49), then he will go down fighting – and may take Aeneas down with him.

50–1 et nos . . ./ spargimus, et nostro . . . de vulnere: the first-person plural forms here are plural for singular; the initial **et** means 'also'.

50 tela . . . ferrumque haud debile: **tela ferrumque** is probably a hendiadys (41–2n.), 'spears with iron points'; **haud debile** is litotes (understatement used for positive affirmation, often, as here, employing a double negative): 'not without force' = 'mighty'. **pater**: 13n. **dextra**: ablative of instrument.

52–3 Turnus' scornful image of Venus concealing Aeneas with a 'womanly cloud' is indebted to a striking scene in the *Iliad*, where Aphrodite (Venus) saves Aeneas from death at the hands of the Greek warrior Diomedes, and Apollo hides him in a cloud – a standard way of making something temporarily invisible in ancient epic (*Iliad* V.311–453).

52   illi: Aeneas (dative, after **longe**). **dea mater**: Venus. **fugacem**: understand *illum* or *Aenean* (object of **tegat**).

53   tegat et . . . occulat: present subjunctives, after **quae** (relative of purpose). **sese**: a variant form of *se*, here referring to Venus herself. **vanis . . . umbris**: ablative of instrument or of place where.

54–5   Only now do we learn that Amata (Latinus' wife) is present, and at 64 that Lavinia is as well (10–80n.). Both women seem to have been present all along (54n.).

54   regina: Queen Amata, wife of Latinus and related (29–30n.) to Turnus. **nova pugnae conterrita sorte**: **nova . . . sorte** is ablative of cause; Amata is frightened by the prospect of Turnus facing Aeneas in single combat (this emotional state implies that she has heard the conversation between Turnus and Latinus, where that prospect has been raised).

55   generum: Turnus; the word is again (31n.) used to mean 'prospective son-in-law' (for Turnus had not married Lavinia). **moritura**: the future participle implies either that something is about to happen, or that something is going to happen at some point; the latter applies here (see XII.593–611). As a result of this advance notice, Amata acquires a tragic quality in this scene.

56–63   The central thrust of Amata's speech is simple, and is simply expressed in line 60: she begs Turnus not to fight.

56   ego te: the verb is **oro** in line 60, which has **ego** as subject, **te** as accusative of the person begged and **unum** (60: 'one thing') as accusative of the thing begged; such extreme hyperbaton is not unusual in entreaties.

AS

56-7   per si quis Amatae/ tangit honos animum: a compressed form of *per honorem tuum Amatae, si quis honos animum tangit*; after **per**, we expect an accusative noun (as in 56 **per has . . . lacrimas**), but Virgil has moved the expected noun into the conditional clause (**si quis Amatae/. . . honos**). Tr. 'by the regard you have for Amata, if any regard touches your mind'.

57-8   spes tu nunc una, senectae/ tu requies miserae: understand *es* with each **tu**.

58-9   decus imperiumque Latini/ te penes: understand *sunt*; **penes** is here (as often) placed after the pronoun which it governs.

59   in te omnis domus inclinata recumbit: 'upon you all our house lies back, having been made to lean'. **domus** here primarily means 'household'; but the imagery of **inclinata recumbit** pictures that royal household as a physical house, leaning dangerously yet held up by a prop (Turnus) which prevents it falling.

60   Teucris: *Teucri* is the word most commonly used to denote the Trojans in the *Aeneid*; they are called 'Teucrians' after one of their earliest ancestors, Teucer, who came from Crete to the Troad (where his daughter married Dardanus: 14–15n.).

61   qui . . . cumque: an instance of tmesis, which is the 'splitting-up' (the Greek verb *tmēgo* means 'I split') of a word for the purpose of effect or utility; in its unsplit form, the word here is *quicumque* (a nominative masculine plural agreeing with **casus**). **isto . . . certamine**: the single combat between Turnus and Aeneas.

62   et me . . . manent: et here means 'also'.

62-3   simul: 'at the same time', that is, as Turnus. **haec invisa relinquam/ lumina**: the light of day (**lumina** is plural for singular), as a privilege enjoyed by the living and not the dead, can stand for life itself; both daylight and life will be loathed by Amata if Turnus should die.

63   nec generum Aenean captiva videbo: Aenean is the accusative form of *Aeneas* (*-n* is a very common accusative ending in Greek); **generum** is a complement to **Aenean**, and **captiva** a complement to the implied *ego* who is the subject of **videbo**. Tr. 'and I will not as a prisoner see Aeneas as my son-in-law'.

64–9 Lavinia (54–5n.) does not speak in this scene, nor, indeed, at any point in the *Aeneid*. But now she does weep and blush, primarily in response to Amata's tearful speech (where the threat of suicide at 62–3 might prompt Lavinia's tears, and the reference to her marriage in 63 might cause her to blush).

64–5   The core of this clause is straightforward enough: *Lavinia vocem matris accepit.* The remaining words **lacrimis . . ./ flagrantes perfusa genas** see a passive participle (**perfusa**: nominative singular, describing Lavinia) followed by an accusative (**flagrantes . . . genas**): this is the so-called 'retained' (or 'Greek') accusative, where the words which would have been accusative as the direct object of an active form of the phrase (in this case, *genas flagrantes lacrimis perfudit*) are kept or 'retained' in the accusative even when the verb is passive; tr. 'her burning cheeks bathed with tears'.

65–6   cui plurimus ignem/ subiecit rubor et calefacta per ora cucurrit: the dative **cui** depends on **subiecit** (lit. 'to whom a very full blush sent up a fire'), but in translation it might best be associated with **ora**: 'a very full blush sent up a fire and ran throughout *her* face, which was made hot'. **ora** is plural for singular.

67–9   A double simile, in which the colour of Lavinia's blushing face is briefly compared to two phenomena quite different from each other: the artificial (**si quis . . .**) process of dyeing ivory red, and the apparently natural juxtaposition of white lilies and red roses.

AS

67–8   Indum . . ./ . . . ebur: the main source of ivory is elephants, and in the Greco-Roman world elephant ivory came mostly from India or North Africa.

67   violaverit: perfect subjunctive (after **si quis**).

68–9   mixta rubent ubi lilia multa/ alba rosa: mixta, lilia and **alba** are all neuter nominative plural; **multa** and **rosa** are feminine ablative singular ('with many a rose').

69   ore: ablative of place where.

70–80   Turnus restates his determination to fight Aeneas; the conversation has not altered his resolve.

70   illum: Turnus (who is the object of **turbat**, but becomes the subject of **figit**, and of **ardet** and **adfatur** in the next line). **figitque in virgine vultus: vultus** is plural for singular. Turnus 'fixes his face on the maiden' – an action presumably indicative of love or even desire (**amor** can denote either emotion).

71   ardet in arma magis: the stiffening of Turnus' resolve seems to follow on from **illum turbat amor** (70); his feelings for Lavinia confirm his determination to fight Aeneas for her hand. **paucisque adfatur:** understand *verbis*.

72–80   Turnus responds to Amata's emotional plea with three emotional lines of his own (72–4), before taking the decisive step of sending a messenger to make arrangements for a single combat against Aeneas (75–80).

72–3   quaeso: parenthetical; literally 'I ask', when accompanying orders or requests the word functions like the English 'please', adding urgency. **ne me . . ./ prosequere: ne** with imperative (**prosequere:** 43n.) to express a negative direct command is an archaism favoured by poets (in classical prose, one expects *noli* with infinitive or *ne* with subjunctive). **omine tanto**: the omen to which Turnus here refers seems to be precisely the tears which he has just mentioned (**lacrimis**) – although it could be (alternatively, or in addition) Amata's strong hints at her own death in lines 62–3. *tantus* means literally 'so great', but translation must often be adapted to suit the noun it modifies: here 'with so terrible an omen'. **in duri certamina Martis euntem: euntem** (masculine accusative singular present participle of *eo*) agrees with **me** in 72. **Martis** may here mean either 'Mars' or 'war' (1n., 790n.).

74   o: 19n. **mater**: 13n. **neque enim Turno mora libera mortis**: understand *est*; literally translated, 'for delay of death is not a matter of free choice for Turnus': that is, 'for Turnus is not free to delay death'. **Turno**: 11n.

75-6   Conceivably, Turnus summons Idmon at this point; but more likely he has been present throughout the conversation (10–80n.). Idmon has no role in the *Aeneid* before this scene or after it; he is presumably a close companion or attendant to Turnus.

75   nuntius: a complement to the implied *tu* who is the subject of **refer** (76). **Phrygio . . . tyranno** refer to Aeneas. Phrygia was an area in central Anatolia, allied to Troy during the Trojan War; 'Phrygian' is thus sometimes used of the Trojans themselves.

76   haud placitura agrees with **dicta** in 75; at XII.107–12, Turnus will be proved wrong about Aeneas' response to his offer.

76-7   caelo: ablative of place where or ablative of route, depending on whether it is taken primarily with **rubebit** or **invecta**. **puniceis invecta rotis Aurora**: the goddess Dawn is imagined as driving a chariot; its wheels are 'scarlet' since the colour of dawn's light is conventionally rosy (cf. **rubebit** 77).

78   non Teucros agat in Rutulos: the unspecified subject of **agat** is Aeneas (the *tyrannus Phrygius* of 75); one expects *ne* with subjunctive

AS

in prohibitions, but **non** can be used when (as here) there is an antithesis between the prohibition and a subsequent clause (in this case, **nostro dirimamus sanguine bellum** 79): 'let him not lead the Trojans against the Rutulians ... [rather,] let us decide the war with our blood'. **Teucrum** is genitive plural: the *-um* ending is an alternative to the usual *-orum*. **quiescant**: jussive subjunctive, as are **dirimamus** (79) and **quaeratur** (80).

79 nostro dirimamus sanguine bellum: the first-person plurals here are probably intended by Turnus as true plurals, referring to both himself and Aeneas.

80 illo ... campo: ablative of place where. The plain is in front of Latinus' city (cf. XII.113–33).

81–106

The conversation of XII.10–80 is now broken off as Turnus moves from determined words to action. The narrator does not show us the response of the other characters present (we next see Latinus at XII.161ff., and Amata and Lavinia only at XII.595–607); he chooses to follow Turnus as he heads into a building or buildings (**tecta** 81: cf. 92–3), which seem to be near Latinus' palace. Here Turnus prepares for the duel with Aeneas by inspecting his horses (82–6), and then by not merely inspecting but putting on his armour and weapons (87–100). Arming scenes are a traditional feature of martial epic, from the *Iliad* onwards. This one is peculiar in its timing: usually such scenes take place immediately prior to a duel or battle, but Turnus here dons his equipment on the evening before the fighting. This is rather odd behaviour; it might be explained by the unstable emotional and mental state apparent in lines 95–100 and especially 101–6.

AS

81   **rapidusque**: adjective used adverbially. **tecta**: 81–106n.

82   **poscit equos**: these are the horses who pull Turnus' chariot (which will be important later: 622n.). **frementes**: the noun which **frementes** describes, *equos*, needs to be supplied from the previous clause (*apo koinou*: 32–3n.). **gaudetque tuens**: 6–7n. **ora**: plural for singular.

83   **Pilumno**: Pilumnus was an Italian fertility god, who is in the *Aeneid* an ancestor of Turnus. **quos ipsa decus dedit Orithyia**: **quos** and **decus** are both accusative, the former as direct object of **dedit**, the latter as a complement ('as a glory'). **Orithyia** was an Athenian princess who was abducted by Boreas (the god of the North Wind) and became his immortal wife; swift horses are naturally associated with the wind, and as a wind divinity Orithyia was able to give Pilumnus the special horses that Turnus has inherited.

84   **qui candore nives anteirent**: an 'explanatory' relative clause, in which a subjunctive verb (**anteirent**) gives the grounds for saying something; this clause explains why the horses were 'a glory': 'since they surpassed …'. **candore** is ablative of respect. **cursibus auras**: *anteirent* is to be understood *apo koinou* (32–3n.). **properi**: the charioteers have responded with alacrity to Turnus' demand (82).

85–6   **lacessunt/pectora plausa**: **lacessunt** probably means 'rouse'; **pectora** means both the horses' chests (when taken with **plausa**) and the horses' hearts (as the object of **lacessunt**). **manibusque …/…cavis**: ablative of instrument.

87   **ipse**: Turnus.

87–8   **auro squalentem alboque orichalco/… loricam**: this *lorica* (corselet) seems to be of the *squamata* type, where multiple metal scales were sewn onto a fabric underlayer; Turnus' corselet is 'rough' (**squalentem**) with gold (**auro** may refer to gold thread or scales)

AS

and with exotic 'orichalc' or mountain copper (scales). This armour covered the body from the lower neck to the upper thigh: Aeneas' spear pierces Turnus' thigh at 904–5 through the edges of his corselet.

88–9　habendo: dative of the gerund, after **aptat** ('he adjusted for wearing'). **rubrae cornua cristae: cornua** are the projecting sockets into which the crest of a helmet is fitted; the 'sockets of the red crest' is an example of *pars pro toto*, where a whole object (here Turnus' helmet) is denoted by reference only to one part of it.

89–90　ensemque . . ./ ensem: the repetition of a word within a sentence (usually after intervening matter) is known as 'epanalepsis'; Virgil likes to use this device to return to an item which has been mentioned briefly, to dwell on it further (as here): this is sometimes termed 'expansion'. Turnus will, in fact, neglect to pick up this sword when he enters battle, to his later cost: see XII.728–45, especially 735–7.

90–1　quem . . . ignipotens deus ipse . . ./ fecerat: the sword handled by Turnus here has the grandest pedigree; Vulcan was the Olympian god of fire and metalworking. Aeneas' whole panoply is made by Vulcan (739n.).

90　Dauno . . . parenti: 22n.

91　candentem agrees with (**ensem**) **quem** ('when it was white hot'). **Stygia . . . unda**: ablative of place where; the Styx was one of the rivers of the underworld. Steel is tempered by being dipped in water.

92–100　Corselet, sword, shield and helmet have been covered in five lines; Turnus' spear is now given nine lines – mixing description and provenance (92–4) with dramatic direct speech (95–100).

92–3　The relative clause (**quae . . ./. . . astabat**) precedes its antecedent (**validam . . . hastam**).

92–3   mediis . . ./ aedibus: ablative of place where; the **aedes** may be identical with the **tecta** of 81, or may be a part of those buildings.

93   vi: ablative of manner.

94   Actoris Aurunci: mentioned in the *Aeneid* only here and in 96 (where **maximus** dignifies Turnus' conquest), Actor is probably an invention of Virgil's. His people, the Aurunci, lived just beyond the southern frontier of Latium. **spolium**: in apposition to **hastam** in 93. **quassatque trementem**: understand *hastam, apo koinou* (32–3n.) from 93. **trementem** is proleptic (that is, it indicates the result of the action of the verb) after **quassat**: 'shook [the spear] so that it was quivering'.

**95–100   **In his enthusiasm for fighting, Turnus speaks aloud to his spear; he even calls on it to help him at 97–100, and the speech contains elements often found in ancient prayers to gods. There may be a hint of blasphemy here: but Turnus' behaviour is perhaps more the product of destabilizing emotion than of long-held convictions (although see 95–6n.).

95–6   o: 19n. **numquam frustrata vocatus/ hasta meos** seems to imply that Turnus has called on his spear like this also in the past. **vocatus** (a noun) is accusative plural.

96–7   te maximus Actor,/ te Turni nunc dextra gerit: with **te maximus Actor** understand *antea gerebat*. **Turni**: 11n.

97–100   da sternere . . ./. . . lacerare . . ./. . . foedare: *do*, meaning 'I grant (someone) the power (to do X),' is followed either by an *ut*-clause or (as here) by an infinitive.

98   loricamque . . . valida lacerare revulsam: Turnus apparently wants to mangle (**lacerare**) Aeneas' *lorica* (87–8n.) after tearing it off (**revulsam**); conceivably he really is keen to disfigure his opponent's

AS

handsome equipment, but this unexpected idea may rather indicate not only brutal violence but also some mental instability. **manu valida**: ablative of instrument, with either **lacerare** or **revulsam** (or both).

99 semiviri Phrygis: Aeneas, who is called *semivir* presumably partly on account of his supposedly effeminate hairstyle (99–100), but also partly because the word **Phrygis** (cf. 75n.) brings to mind the famous Phrygian cult of Cybele, whose priests were eunuchs.

99–100 foedare in pulvere crines/ vibratos calido ferro murraque madentes: the defiling of Aeneas' hair in the dust would follow naturally upon his body being laid low on the ground (**sternere corpus** 97); Turnus probably envisages himself dragging off his enemy's corpse. The sense is complete at the end of 99; line 100 adds a slur on Aeneas, claiming that his hair has had artificial cosmetic treatment – 'curled' with hot tongs and drenched in perfume.

101 his agitur furiis: Turnus' words in 95–100, and probably his actions in 92–5 also, are retrospectively (**his**) characterized as signs of 'frenzy'; the passive **agitur** suggests that Turnus is the victim of violent forces beyond his control.

101–2 totoque ardentis ab ore/ scintillae absistunt, oculis micat acribus ignis: with **ardentis**, understand *Turni*; **oculis . . . acribus** is ablative either of place where or origin. This line and a half is usually taken as metaphor; but **totoque . . . ab ore/ scintillae absistunt** is less easy to accommodate to a purely metaphorical reading than **ardentis** or **oculis micat acribus ignis**. If this is an image, then it is (as the Victorian commentator Page said) 'letting metaphor run riot'. The alternative is to consider the possibility that literal sparks 'burst forth from the whole face' of Turnus, which would be extraordinary. Either way, the striking language raises questions about Turnus' mental and emotional stability at this point.

103–6 Turnus is compared to a bull who is about to fight a 'battle'. The main point of comparison is the restless, angry energy of both figures. The bull's opponent is not here specified, but the natural candidate is another bull; this is made more likely by the content of the related simile at XII.715–22.

103–4 **mugitus**: accusative plural. **prima in proelia**: 'for the beginning of the battle'.

104 **irasci in cornua temptat**: *irascor* means 'I am angry' or 'I become angry', but by following the verb with **in cornua** Virgil here extends its usage to mean something like 'I throw my rage (into)'.

105 **trunco**: dative after **obnixus**.

106 **sparsa . . . harena**: ablative absolute; the scattering of sand is a by-product of the bull's violent movements.

107–613: Turnus' offer to fight in single combat is welcomed by Aeneas, and the following morning preparations are made for this. But Juno encourages Turnus' sister Juturna to disrupt the preparations. Fighting between Trojans and Italians breaks out once again, and Aeneas is hit by an arrow and forced to withdraw. In his absence Turnus joins battle, initially with great success. But Aeneas is healed and returns to the field; Turnus is kept away from him by Juturna, and Aeneas reluctantly attacks Latinus' city in an attempt to finish the war quickly.

A more detailed summary of the content of these lines is on pp. 11–12.

614–80

After the delay and disruption of the planned single combat between Aeneas and Turnus, this scene brings that combat back into prospect.

AS

It takes place on the edge of the plain on which the battle is being fought (614). From here, Turnus hears unnerving noises from Latinus' city; he then receives a spoken report explaining what is happening there. Stunned by what he learns, he resolves finally to face Aeneas.

614   interea: Turnus has not featured in the narrative since line 553; in the meantime, Aeneas has attacked Latinus' city and Amata has committed suicide. Lines 614–16 give us an idea of what Turnus has been doing while these events took place. **extremo . . . in aequore**: Turnus has been driven away from more dangerous territory by Juturna (a process begun at XII.467–85).

615–16   iam . . ./ iam mark a contrast with Turnus' alacrity earlier, most notably soon after Aeneas was shot (XII.324–82). **successu**: ablative of cause.

617–19   Unsettling noises from the city reach Turnus' ears. We are told this twice, in different ways – first, **attulit hunc illi caecis terroribus aura/ commixtum clamorem**, then **arrectasque impulit aures/ confusae sonus urbis et inlaetabile murmur**. This technique of presenting an event or piece of information twice, often from varying aspects, is favoured by Virgil; it is sometimes called 'theme and variation'. Here, its deployment focuses our attention on this significant moment in the plot; for Turnus' realization of what is happening at the city will drive him back to face Aeneas in the decisive single combat.

617–18   attulit hunc illi caecis terroribus aura/ commixtum clamorem: with the word order simplified, *aura hunc clamorem terroribus caecis commixtum illi attulit*. **illi**: dative, and referring to Turnus. **clamorem**: primarily that of Latinus' frightened citizens as the Trojans besiege their city, but also that of the people of the court responding to Amata's suicide. **caecis terroribus**: ablative dependent on **commixtum** ('mixed up with terrors without clear cause').

618   arrectasque ... aures: Turnus' ears are literally 'pricked up', and so 'listening'.

619   confusae sonus urbis et inlaetabile murmur clarify the nature of the **clamorem** mentioned in 618.

620–1   Turnus' speech is only brief. He will reflect at greater length in lines 632–49, when he has collected his thoughts; at this stage, he is unnerved and confused. The two questions he asks exhibit the 'theme and variation' technique observed in 617–19n.

620   tanto ... luctu: ablative of means.

621   quisve ruit tantus ... clamor: *-ve* is used here to 'link questions, with cumulative effect' (*OLD* 3); tr. 'and'.

622   adductisque ... subsistit habenis: Turnus has been fighting from a chariot ever since he joined the battle (XII.324ff.). The chariot was being driven by Juturna (623–4n.); here at 622 Turnus has presumably seized the reins himself.

623–30   Juturna is a water-nymph (885–6n.) and Turnus' sister. Mentioned only once in the *Aeneid* before Book XII (at X.439), she plays a considerable part in the final movement of the poem, intervening in the action and trying to keep her brother safe. She was last directly mentioned at XII.485, but has been driving Turnus' chariot since XII.471 (in disguise: 623–4n.). Here she has divined from his words and actions in 620–2 that her brother is contemplating changing course; she tries to pre-empt this by presenting arguments for continuing to act as they have been doing.

623–5   atque huic .../.../ talibus occurrit dictis: the subject of **occurrit** is Juturna (the **soror** referred to in the *ut*-clause), **huic** the dative object (referring to Turnus). **talibus ... dictis**: ablative of instrument.

623-4   in faciem soror ut conversa Metisci/ aurigae currumque et equos et lora regebat: the word order is not straightforward, with **ut** (causal 'as': *OLD* 21) postponed from its expected position at the start of the clause, and **in faciem** moved forward from a position between **conversa** and **Metisci**. **in faciem ... conversa**: **conversa** here is a so-called middle-passive, meaning not so much 'having been turned' as a more reflexive 'having turned herself' (cf. 784, 862, 865). Juturna's adoption of Metiscus' appearance, and her seizure of his role as Turnus' charioteer, was described at XII.467-72.

625-30   Juturna speaks as Metiscus; no element in the speech gives away her true identity.

625-6   hac .../... qua: 'in this direction ... where'.

625   sequamur: jussive subjunctive.

626   prima viam victoria pandit: **prima** functions as an adverb (as if *primum*); Turnus' 'victory at first opened up a way' (presumably by cutting down any Trojans in his path). The narrative of 614-16 (cf. 664) shows that Turnus' 'victories' are by this stage only modest.

627   Juturna's claim in this line will shortly be undermined by Saces (XII.653, 661-4). **sunt alii qui ... possint**: the subjunctive is often found in a relative clause after an indefinite antecedent; tr. 'there are others who are able'. **manu**: 23n.

628   Italis: dative after **ingruit**. A considerable number of Aeneas' own troops are in fact Italian (namely, the very substantial forces from Etruria fighting with the Trojans as allies: VIII.475-513, X.148-214); but 'Italians' is used fairly frequently in the *Aeneid* to denote the combined army of the Latins and their many allies from central and southern Italy ('catalogued' at VII.641-817).

AS

629 et nos: Juturna argues that just as Aeneas is killing Italians (628), so, too, Turnus must kill Trojans. **mittamus**: jussive subjunctive. **manu**: 23n.

630 numero and **honore** are both ablative of respect. **honore** is qualified by the genitive **pugnae** ('honour in battle'); **numero** requires *funerorum* to be supplied (after 629 **funera**), or a word indicating 'victims'.

631 This is one of fifty to sixty (the exact number is disputed) metrically incomplete lines in the transmitted text of the *Aeneid*. It is generally agreed that their presence indicates that Virgil had not quite applied the finishing touches to the poem when he died in 19 BC (see pp. 2–3). Some such lines have a certain appeal in their unfinished state; but others, including this one, lack any artistic qualities. An ancient biography of Virgil claims that when composing, the poet would sometimes insert 'stop-gap' phrases in his narrative so that he could move briskly on to a subsequent section without losing his inspiration (Donatus *Vita* 24); this seems a plausible explanation for the nature and content of line 631.

Turnus ad haec: a verb of speaking is missing.

632–49 Turnus rejects his sister's proposal. He does not yet spell out an alternative course of action; but in his determination to show that he is neither a coward nor indifferent to his comrades' suffering, and in his acceptance of the possibility that he may die, he clearly hints at the resolve which is made explicit later in the scene (676–80).

632 o: 19n. **soror**: Turnus immediately shows the disguised Juturna that he knows her true identity.

632–4 et dudum agnovi . . ./. . ./ et nunc nequiquam fallis dea: the construction emphasizes Juturna's total failure to deceive her brother, both now and previously. **agnovi**: understand *te* as the object.

632–3   cum prima per artem/ foedera turbasti teque haec in bella dedisti: the past-tense verbs in this *cum*-clause are indicative because the clause is 'determinative' – that is, it identifies the time at which the action of the main clause (632 **dudum agnovi**) took place. The events to which Turnus here refers are narrated at XII.222–88: Juturna disguised herself as the Italian Camers and encouraged the Latin soldiers to fight (regardless of the treaty), then sent a misleading bird-omen which prompted the augur Tolumnius to attack Aeneas' men.

632   prima: adverbial (cf. 626n.). **per artem:** *ars* seems to mean 'trick' or 'stratagem' here, given Juturna's use of disguise and her sending of the misleading omen (632–3n.).

633   turbasti: a 'syncopated' form of *turbavisti*. **foedera ... bella:** both plural for singular.

634   nequiquam fallis dea: lit. 'in vain you escape notice as a goddess'; tr. 'you do not succeed in hiding your divinity'.

634–5   sed quis ...: Turnus assumes (correctly) that his sister has not been acting on her own initiative; we know from XII.134–60 that Juno was the instigator.

635   demissam: agrees with **te**. **labores:** 'struggles' (*labor* implies effort, or suffering, or both).

636   letum: Turnus assumes the likelihood of his own death. This suggests that he is already, consciously or subconsciously, anticipating a decisive duel with Aeneas (cf. 643–9); for there is no immediate danger of death at present.

637   nam quid ago?: in deliberative questions the verb can be either subjunctive or (as here) indicative. **nam** follows logically on **letum** in the previous line; the train of thought seems to be: 'have you really come to witness my death? – since you will witness my death, for what can I do to avoid that?'. **aut quae iam spondet Fortuna salutem?**: Fortuna was worshipped at Rome from an early stage, and in Virgil's day there were a number of temples associated with the goddess in and around the city. Fortuna could take various guises; Turnus here asks which of these guarantees his safety. Given **letum** in 636, the answer he expects seems to be 'none'.

638–40   vidi. . ./ Murranum . . ./ oppetere: accusative and infinitive after a verb of perception (**vidi**). The remaining elements of the sentence fill out a picture of Murranus: **vocantem**, **ingentem** and **victum** all agree with **Murranum**, and **quo** (introducing the relative clause in 639) refers to him. Although close to Turnus (639), Murranus is not an important figure in the *Aeneid*: he is mentioned only here and at XII.529–34 (see 640n.).

638   me voce vocantem: 'calling me aloud' – literally, 'calling me with a call'. Such a combination of cognate words of different type (typically, verb and noun) is termed a *figura etymologica*.

639   quo: ablative of comparison.

640   ingenti vulnere victum: Murranus' wounding is narrated at XII.529–34. Aeneas hurls a rock which knocks him from his chariot onto the ground; there, he is trampled by his own horses. That he went on to die from the wounds he suffered is confirmed here.

641   occidit infelix ... Ufens: Ufens was leader of the Aequi (VII.744–9) and a significant figure in the Italian war effort (VIII.6–8), whose death (hence **infelix** here) at the hands of the Trojan Gyas is mentioned very briefly at XII.460.

641–2   ne nostrum dedecus . . ./ aspiceret: a purpose clause. Turnus imagines Ufens as dying so as not to witness Turnus' dishonour (**nostrum** is plural for singular). This was clearly not the case; but the word **dedecus** indicates how Turnus views his own recent conduct (it

AS

also prepares us for the change of direction which becomes clear over the next seven lines of his speech).

642   Teucri potiuntur corpore et armis: Turnus mentions this as a further reproach to himself. The enemy not only killed his comrade – they also possess his body (depriving Ufens of burial, at least for now) and his arms (winning honour for themselves, and dishonour for those who failed to prevent this).

643–4   exscindine domos .../ perpetiar: accusative and infinitive dependent upon **perpetiar**. Turnus seems to intuit something of what is happening to Latinus' city from the noises heard at 617–21; Saces will shortly confirm some of his fears (654–6).

643   id ... unum refers to the idea *exscindi domos*. **rebus**: dative, depending on **defuit**. Tr. 'that was the one thing the situation lacked'; the statement is bitterly ironic.

644   dextra nec Drancis dicta refellam?: **dextra** is ablative of instrument. Drances is a statesman who, at the council in Book XI (see p. 10), argued that the war was Turnus' fault, blamed him for losses incurred in battle and criticized him for cowardice in refusing to fight Aeneas on the battlefield or in a duel. Turnus' naming of Drances here shows that at least some of these criticisms have rankled; to judge from 645–9, it is the charge of cowardice which he plans to refute by his actions.

645   terga dabo et Turnum fugientem haec terra videbit?: the same action is presented from two different perspectives ('theme and variation': 617–19n.). **terga**: plural for singular. **Turnum**: 11n.

646   usque adeone mori miserum est?: 'is it so very wretched a thing to die?'. Turnus' question is the climax of the train of thought underlying lines 636–45: he has recognized many reasons for fighting Aeneas, and now disposes of the main objection (that death might result).

AS

646-7 vos o mihi, Manes,/ este boni: the *Manes* were underworld divinities understood as the deified dead, who were an important element in Roman domestic religion; Turnus asks for their favour (**este** is the second-person plural imperative of *sum*). Line 649 suggests that he is thinking in particular of the dead members of his own family. **o**: 19n.

647 quoniam superis aversa voluntas: understand *est*. **superis** is dative: the usage is an extension of the possessive dative. Tr. 'since the will of the gods is hostile'. This is the first time in the *Aeneid* that Turnus suspects that the gods may not be on his side (previously he has been confident, sometimes bullishly so); he returns to the point at 676 and 895.

648-9 ad vos: Turnus continues to address the *Manes*. **anima** is a complement to the implied *ego* who is the subject of **descendam**. **istius inscia culpae**: 'not knowing that sense of guilt', or perhaps 'innocent of that wrongdoing' – either way, **istius ... culpae** refers to the behaviour rejected by Turnus in lines 643-5.

650 ecce: Virgil uses this interjection in passages of vivid narrative to introduce a new event, especially a sudden or surprising one: it is probably best translated 'look!' (however unnatural this may seem at first). **medios ... per hostes**: Saces has shown bravery and perhaps desperation in getting through to Turnus; it seems from his speech that he has come either from Latinus' city itself or from the fighting around it.

651 vectus equo: when the meaning is clear, poets often omit a preposition which one would expect to be present in classical prose ([*in*] *equo* here). **spumante**: 'foaming', that is, at the mouth – from exertion. **Saces**: not previously mentioned in the *Aeneid*, and not mentioned again once he has finished his speech (653-64).

AS

651–2   adversa . . ./. . . ora: accusative of respect after **saucius** (5n.); tr. 'wounded full in the face'. **sagitta**: ablative of instrument.

653–64   Saces reports what has happened in and around Latinus' city in Turnus' absence. It is a memorable speech – urgent, forceful and (by line 664) blunt.

653   in te suprema salus: understand *est*. **miserere tuorum**: 43n. Masculine plural forms of *tuus* without a noun mean 'your men' or 'your people'.

654   Aeneas fulminat: a *fulmen* is a thunderbolt or lightning-strike, which are the weapons used by Jupiter; **fulminat** is therefore an extremely strong image for Aeneas' performance on the battlefield, and shows the terrifying impression he has made on the Latin forces; cf. 700. **armis**: ablative of instrument, after **fulminat**.

654–5   summasque minatur/ deiecturum arces Italum excidioque daturum: understand *se* and *esse* with both **deiecturum** and **daturum**; the construction is accusative and future infinitive, as expected after a verb of threatening. **Italum**: genitive plural (78n.); on the name, cf. 628n. Saces' account of Aeneas' threats is confirmed by Aeneas' own speech at XII.565–73 (cf. 762). **arces**: the plural looks like hyperbole, but is also found at XII.698; Latinus' city may be imagined as having more than one fortified high point.

656   faces ad tecta volant: again Saces' report is supported by the narrative elsewhere (XII.596 *ignes ad tecta volare*; cf. XII.573 *ferte faces*).

656–7   in te ora Latini,/ in te oculos referunt: *os* (accusative plural *ora*) can mean 'face' (*OLD* 6) or 'gaze' (*OLD* 10); the former is preferable here, producing along with **oculos** a kind of 'theme and variation' (617–19n.) instead of a simple tautology.

AS

657-8 Once the treaty has been broken in Book XII, Latinus is relegated to the margins both of Virgil's narrative and of the power struggle between the Trojans and the Latins. The king flees as fighting breaks out (285-6); between then and now, he is glimpsed only at 609-11 (a dejected, broken figure, 'with clothing ripped, stunned at the fate of his wife and the fall of his city, befouling his grey hair overspread with filthy dust'). Here at 657-8, he seems to imagine that his authority might yet count for something; by 707-9, his impotence is obvious.

658   quos generos vocet aut quae sese ad foedera flectat: indirect questions, introduced by **mussat** in 657. Latinus is presented as considering two separate questions, but they amount to the same thing (insofar as the identity of his son-in-law will determine the nature of the treaty made). The plurals **generos** and **foedera** are surprising, and may simply be instances of plural for singular; but in the case of **generos**, at any rate, it may be that Latinus envisages not only the individual leaders (Aeneas and Turnus) as potential sons-in-law, but also (in a less literal sense) their followers. **sese**: 53n.

659-60   regina . . . dextra/ occidit ipsa sua: Amata's death is narrated at XII.595-603. There the means of her suicide is specified as hanging; Saces' **dextra/. . . sua** (ablative of instrument) leaves this unclear. **tui** is objective genitive after **fidissima**: 'most loyal to you'; the queen's devotion to Turnus was visible in lines 54-63, and at XII.595-600 her (mistaken) belief that Turnus is dead is a key factor in her suicide.

660   lucemque: 'life' (cf. 62-3n. on *lumina*). **exterrita**: it is not clear how (or, indeed, whether) Saces has gained accurate information about Amata's motives in taking her life; but he assumes that fear was important, and XII.595-600 broadly confirm this (cf. 62-3).

661   pro portis: the gates of Latinus' city; the Trojans had launched attacks there as they began their assault on the city (XII.577).

AS

Messapus et acer Atinas: Atinas is mentioned only twice in the
Aeneid – here, and at XI.869 (where he is also **acer**). Messapus is
a much more notable figure. First introduced at VII.691–705 as
commander of the allied Faliscan contingent, he becomes one of the
most important leaders and warriors on the Latin side; in Book XII,
he is second in visibility and importance only to Turnus among the
Italians on the battlefield. This is his final appearance in the epic.

662   acies: accusative plural, referring to the Trojans and their allies.

663–4   strictisque seges mucronibus horret/ ferrea: 'an iron crop
bristles with drawn swords'. The soldiers facing Messapus and Atinas
are pictured as a metaphorical **seges**, probably here a crop of wheat:
the most obvious points of comparison are the dense ranks of the
plants in a wheatfield (cf. **densae** 663), and their tall pointed ears
(cf. **strictis . . . mucronibus**). The crop is **ferrea** because the soldiers
wear iron armour. **seges . . . horret/ ferrea. tu currum . . . versas**:
asyndeton between clauses can be used to emphasize a contrast
('adversative' asyndeton); when translating into English, the insertion
of 'but' may be necessary to convey the effect.

664   tu: Saces addresses Turnus, but we know that it is Juturna who
has been driving the chariot and keeping her brother on the margins
of the battlefield.

665–71   Virgil presents in some detail the immediate and shattering
psychological impact of Saces' words upon Turnus.

665   obstipuit denotes a state of mental and physical shock,
characterized by the temporary incapacity of some or all of the senses;
sometimes in the *Aeneid*, the verb and its cognates indicate merely the
loss of speech ('dumbstruck') or an individual being more generally
'astounded', but Turnus here seems to suffer something more profound
(cf. 669n.). **varia confusus imagine rerum**: 'overwhelmed by the

AS

complex representation of the situation'. **imagine** (ablative of means) refers to the account provided by Saces' speech.

666   obtutu tacito: 'with a silent, fixed gaze'; such a description of one sensory activity (**obtutu**) in terms appropriate to another (**tacito**) is known as 'synaesthesia'.

666-8   Turnus experiences a violent seething (**aestuat** 666) of different feelings: shame (**pudor**), which we have already seen (632-49) arising from his knowledge that he has not done all he could to help his comrades on the battlefield; madness (**insania**), the source of which is less obvious (simply battle rage, or something with deeper roots?) – unless it is a product of the grief 'mixed in' with it; grief (**luctu**), in response to the news of Amata's suicide but perhaps also to deaths of comrades (cf. 638-42); love (**amor**) for Lavinia: that this is 'troubled' or perhaps 'stimulated' by frenzy (**furiis**) may suggest Turnus sees the news in lines 657-8 as threatening his hopes; last, **conscia virtus**, probably 'courage conscious of itself' but possibly 'courage conscious of guilt'.

666   ingens: the adjective agrees with **pudor**, but commentators have generally regarded the adjective as adverbial, qualifying **aestuat**.

669   ut primum discussae umbrae et lux reddita menti: with **discussae** and **reddita** understand *sunt* and *est*, respectively. The language of darkness and light may indicate that Turnus experiences some sort of literal 'blackout' under the psychological pressures described in lines 666-8; alternatively, Virgil pictures a metaphorical storm of emotion bringing clouds of darkness into Turnus' mind – which are eventually dispelled sufficiently for some daylight to return. Literal or metaphorical, the diction conveys the overwhelming nature of the experience.

670-1   Saces' report was largely concerned with events in and around Latinus' city, and it is naturally in that direction that Turnus

AS

now turns his gaze. 670–1 use the 'theme and variation' technique
(617–19n.) to dwell on an action which will have decisive consequences
for Turnus himself and for the plot of the poem.

670   ardentes applied to Turnus' eyeballs could be metaphorical, or
more literal (cf. 101–2n.).

672–5   Turnus' gaze settles on a defensive tower – not previously
mentioned in the poem – in the construction of which he was (we
learn here) closely involved. The tower is mobile (675), and is used to
transport troops to various parts of the city wall (they cross from
tower to wall using the **pontes** of 675). Placed just inside the wall, it
has been hit by a firebrand (cf. 656n.); the flames have swept up the
wooden frame, level by level (672).

672   ecce: 650n.

672–3   flammis inter tabulata volutus/. . . vertex: 'a whirling
column of fire, having rolled with flames from level to level'. **vertex**
denotes something which twists or whirls around. **volutus** means
'having rolled (itself)' (the passive of *volvo* can be used in a 'middle' or
quasi-reflexive sense). **flammis** is, in part, ablative of means (the
column has rolled itself upwards by means of the flames catching),
but also loosely helps to define the meaning of **vertex** (a column
whirling with flames). **undabat:** Virgil likes to describe the action of
fire using terms more obviously appropriate to liquids.

673–4   turrimque . . ./ turrim . . . quam eduxerat: 89–90n.

674   ipse: Turnus.

676–80   Turnus' speech is an immediate response to the sight of the
burning tower, but also a slightly delayed reaction to Saces' report. It is
clear that what he has learned has confirmed and stiffened the resolve
already suggested in his previous speech to Juturna (632–49n.), and
convinced him that he must act now.

676   iam iam: the reduplication adds urgency; tr. 'already now'. **absiste morari**: an accusative object for **morari** must be understood – probably *fata*, but possibly *me*.

677   quo deus et quo dura vocat Fortuna: understand *vocat* with **quo deus** (*apo koinou*: 32–3n.). **deus** is unspecific, perhaps reflecting Turnus' increasing awareness of the limits of his knowledge of the divine dimension to the action (647n.); but Virgil can be similarly unspecific at times as a narrator. **sequamur**: jussive subjunctive, and probably a genuine plural (including both Juturna and Turnus).

678   stat conferre manum Aeneae: understand *mihi* after **stat**, which means 'it is (my) fixed resolve (to do X)'. **Aeneae** is dative after **conferre manum**.

678–9   stat quidquid acerbi est/ morte pati: again, understand *mihi* after **stat**. **quidquid** followed by a partitive genitive and **est** means literally, 'whatever there is of X'; here, and often, it expresses the idea 'all of X'. **quidquid** is a relative pronoun, and neuter nominative singular: strictly speaking, an antecedent *id* (accusative singular object of **pati**) should be understood, but, in practice, the antecedent to forms of *quisquis* is very frequently omitted (cf. 12n.). **morte** is both ablative of means with **pati** and ablative of place where with **quidquid acerbi est**. Tr. 'I am resolved to suffer in death all its bitterness.'

679–80   indecorem is a complement to **me**.

680   hunc . . . sine me furere ante furorem: **me furere** is accusative and infinitive after **sine** (25n.). **hunc . . . furorem** is the object of **furere**: a striking *figura etymologica* (638n.) emphasizing by repetition the element of irrationality in Turnus' action, or perhaps in himself. (**hunc** refers primarily to the decision confirmed in 678–9, which Turnus knows is likely to result in his death and which in that sense can be regarded as 'mad' – and might well be so regarded by Juturna.

AS

But **hunc** may alternatively, or additionally, refer to a *furor* which Turnus recognizes as a characteristic of his, natural or imposed upon him, and which he sees manifested in the course he is now embarking upon.) **ante**: adverb ('beforehand'); Turnus presumably means 'before I die', but avoids specifying so unappealing a prospect.

681–709

Turnus' resolution is put into action: he rushes across the battlefield to face Aeneas (681–96). Aeneas' reaction is presented in comparable terms (701–3n.). Fighting elsewhere ceases as everyone turns to watch the single combat (704–9).

681   **arvis**: the dative is used by poets to express 'place whither'.

682–3   maestamque sororem/ deserit: as we discover at 784–5, Juturna does not accept being left behind; it will require Jupiter's intervention to dissuade her from continuing to help her brother (843–86).

683   rapido cursu: 'at a swift run'. **media agmina rumpit**: the 'lines of troops' seem to be both Turnus' own men and **hostes** (682); Turnus rushes through the fighting which is taking place between the outskirts of the battlefield and the city.

684–9 Turnus' movement across the battlefield is compared to that of a great rock crashing down a mountainside.

684–5   veluti montis saxum de vertice praeceps/ cum ruit: montis is possessive genitive after **vertice**; the adjective **praeceps** agrees with **saxum** but should be taken adverbially with **ruit**.

685–6   avulsum vento gives the immediate occasion for the dislodging of the rock; **seu turbidus imber/ proluit aut annis solvit**

sublapsa vetustas offers two different explanations for the weak attachment of the rock to the mountain. **proluit** and **solvit** are both perfect tense. **annis . . . sublapsa vetustas**: 'age which has slipped in with the years' (**annis** is ablative of means: it is by means of the passing years that age has slipped in).

687 **fertur in abruptum magno mons improbus actu**: 'the mountain is carried straight down, relentlessly, with mighty impulse'. **mons** is striking hyperbole for **saxum**. **improbus** denotes action which is persistent and shows no regard for others: the adjective agrees with **mons** but should be taken adverbially with **fertur**.

688 **exsultatque solo**: **solo** is ablative of place where or route ('over the ground': 76–7n.).

690–1 **ubi plurima fuso/ sanguine terra madet**: **plurima** agrees with **terra**, but should be understood adverbially with **madet**; **fuso/ sanguine** is ablative of means or cause, explaining **madet**. The abundant blood on the ground towards the walls has been shed during fighting which followed the Trojan assault on Latinus' city. The progress of that assault beyond its initial stages (XII.574–86) is not directly narrated; but Saces' speech has given a powerful impression of aspects of it, and the ferocity of the battle is suggested by **plurima . . ./ . . . madet** here.

691 **striduntque hastilibus aurae**: 'the air was whirring with spears'; the expression is a little unexpected, insofar as it is really the spears which are whirring in the air.

692 **manu**: ablative of instrument with **significat**. **incipit** can be used elliptically to mean 'he begins to speak'.

693–5 A brief speech (this is not the time for a lengthy address), of instruction (693) and explanation (694–5).

693   parcite: *parco* generally governs a verb in the infinitive or a noun in the dative indicating what the subject is refraining from doing, but occasionally (as here) it is used elliptically on its own; that Turnus is asking the Rutulians to refrain from fighting is obvious from his instruction to the Latins in the second half of the line.

694   quaecumque est fortuna, mea est: the antecedent (**fortuna**) is attracted into the relative clause (48–9n.).

694–5   me verius unum/ pro vobis foedus luere et decernere ferro: with **verius** (here neuter nominative singular comparative adjective: 'more just'), understand *est*; that phrase is followed by an accusative (**me … unum**) and infinitives (**luere** and **decernere**). **foedus luere** literally means 'to atone for the treaty': Turnus presumably means 'to atone for the breaking of the treaty' (his elliptical formulation avoids explicit reference to wrongdoing). **ferro** (16n.): ablative of instrument with **decernere**.

696   discessere … dedere: 12n.

697   pater Aeneas: Aeneas is the metaphorical father of the Trojan people whom he leads – and of the Romans in the future (at XII.166 he is described as *pater Aeneas, Romanae stirpis origo* – 'founder of the Roman race').

698   muros et summas … arces: Aeneas was last the focus of the narrative at XII.579–82, as the assault on the walls of Latinus' city began; since then, references in speeches have reminded us of his involvement in the fighting there (628, 654–5). **arces**: 654–5n.

699   praecipitatque moras omnes: 'and threw aside all delays'. **opera omnia rumpit**: **omnia** implies that the Trojan assault on Latinus' city is at this point entirely halted, and after 706–7 nothing in the remainder of the epic suggests otherwise. The combat between Aeneas and Turnus will decide the outcome of the war; the attention of the poet, and of his characters (704–9), is henceforth entirely directed towards that.

700   **laetitia**: ablative of cause, with **exsultans**. Aeneas is consistently portrayed as trying to avoid full-scale war (cf. XII.109, 311–17, 464–7, 481–99, 572–3, 580–2), and he is now delighted at finally being able to fight Turnus – not because he is bloodthirsty, but rather because he has an opportunity to bring an end to the war. **horrendumque**: the accusative of a neuter adjective can be used adverbially; tr. 'and terrifyingly'. **intonat armis**: cf. 654n.

701–3   Aeneas is compared to three mountains (the third of which, in Italy, is given the most extended description). The simile primarily illustrates the frightening grandeur of the Trojan himself and of the noise made by his weapons. The lines balance (and in their hyperbole clearly outdo) the comparison of Turnus to a *montis saxum de vertice* at 684–9.

701–3   **quantus Athos aut quantus Eryx aut ipse .../... quantus .../... pater Appenninus**: an abbreviated form of a comparative sentence with correlative adjectives (19–21n.); understand *(Aeneas) tantus erat* at the beginning, and *est* after each **quantus**: '[Aeneas was] as great as Athos [is] or as great as Eryx [is] or as great as father Appenninus himself [is] ...'

701   **Athos**: a mountain on the eastern side of the Chalcidice Peninsula in the northern Aegean. **Eryx**: a mountain just inland from the western coast of Sicily, a little north of the town of Drepanum.

701–3   The word introducing the third comparison (**quantus**) is delayed into line 702, and the subject of the clause thus introduced is delayed even further, into line 703 (**pater Appenninus**) – although **ipse** in 701 does prepare us for it. With word order simplified, the start of the clause would read: *quantus ipse pater Appenninus [est], cum ...*

701-2   coruscis/. . .ilicibus: ablative of means with **fremit**; a roaring sound comes from the mountain when wind blows through the leaves of the oak trees growing on its slopes. **coruscis** indicates quivering movement, or flickering light, or (as here) both: the leaves of the holm oak (*ilex*) quiver in the wind and seem to flash, since they are dark on one side and lighter on the other.

702-3   gaudetque .../. . . se attollens: 6-7n. **nivali/ vertice se attollens . . . ad auras**: **nivali/ vertice** is ablative of means, explaining how the mountain might be regarded as rising up towards the air of the sky.

703   pater Appenninus: the Apennine mountain range runs down the middle of Italy; in speaking of one peak, Virgil probably has in mind the highest part of the range, the massif known nowadays as Gran Sasso.

704-5   omnes/. . . Itali: 628n. **convertere**: 12n.

705-6   quique alta tenebant/ moenia quique imos pulsabant ariete muros: the two clauses specify respectively defenders of Latinus' city and men assaulting it.

707   armaque deposuere umeris: the gesture marks the end of the fighting, for all except Turnus and Aeneas (cf. 699n.). **deposuere**: 11-12n.

707-9   stupet .../. . ./ inter se coiisse viros: the construction is accusative and infinitive after **stupet** ('was dumbstruck (to see) that the men had joined battle'). That verb has the same root as **obstipuit** (665n.); Latinus is stunned by awe at the size of the combatants (**ingentes** 708) and the international scale of the war (708), but also perhaps by sadness – or even horror – that the duel which he once tried to avert (cf. 19-45) is now imminent (709). **ipse Latinus**: the king provides a grand climax to Virgil's survey of the spectators (cf. 704–6); but he is as passive and powerless as the others looking on (657–8n.). This is his final appearance in the *Aeneid*.

708   diversis partibus: ablative of place where, after **genitos. orbis**: partitive genitive. **orbis** identifies a global dimension for the combat; **diversis partibus** may encourage us to think in terms of East and West, or perhaps of Asia and Europe: Aeneas was born in the Troad, and Turnus (we assume) at Ardea.

709   coiisse: the tense is a little surprising (given that the first moves in the single combat are only narrated in the following line); perhaps Virgil wishes to indicate that while he has been describing the onlookers, Turnus and Aeneas have come close enough to each other to start fighting.

710–27

The single combat begins with ferocious violence and loud noise. This is the first time Aeneas and Turnus have fought each other: at this stage, the contest seems an even one. On the structure of 710–952, see pp. 16–17.

710   atque: 'and indeed'; Virgil confirms in direct narrative what we have glimpsed through the eyes of Latinus (709n.). **illi**: Aeneas and Turnus. **vacuo ... aequore**: ablative of place where. **patuerunt ... campi** may simply be a variation on that same theme of emptiness (617–19n.), but in the light of 896–8 below **campi** might be understood as more or less identifiable sub-divisions of that larger *aequor*. At any rate, repetition of the idea of emptiness emphasizes that the withdrawing armies have left a large space for Aeneas and Turnus. Tr. 'when the fields lay open on the empty plain'.

AS

711   **procursu rapido**: cf. 683n. **coniectis eminus hastis**: the standard opening act in a formal duel in ancient heroic epic. Virgil passes over the moment swiftly (contrast 919–23), and at this stage gives no indication of where either spear goes (contrast 923–7): clearly, each has missed its target. The spear thrown by Aeneas reappears, somewhat unexpectedly, later in the narrative (766–90 and 887ff.).

712   **Martem**: metonymy for 'battle' or 'fighting' (1n.). **clipeis atque aere sonoro**: hendiadys (41–2n.), meaning 'with the bronze of their shields clanging loud'. The ablatives are at least in part instrumental (not merely 'attendant circumstances'): the warriors charge into combat using their shields, as well as their swords (713–14), as offensive equipment; cf. 724.

713   **dat gemitum tellus**: presumably under the weight of the huge (**ingentes** 708) warriors; there is some hyperbole here.

713–14   **crebros ensibus ictus/ congeminant**: having thrown their spears, Aeneas and Turnus fight at close quarters with swords (**ensibus**: ablative of instrument with **congeminant**).

714   **fors et virtus miscentur in unum**: literally, 'chance and courage were mixed together into one thing'. Given that the clause follows in asyndeton upon **crebros ensibus ictus/ congeminant**, Virgil seems to be indicating an outcome of the sheer number of blows there emphasized: 'they set to with such fury that the effects of chance and valour became undistinguishable' (Maguinness).

715–22   Turnus and Aeneas are compared to a pair of bulls fighting violently – and loudly – for control of a herd. (Turnus is compared to a bull in a related simile earlier in the book: 103–6n.)

715–19   Line 715 sets the scene for the action of the simile (4n.); the temporal clause in 716–17 (**cum .../... incurrunt**) is followed by three main clauses, although it may be best to regard **pavidi cessere magistri** as parenthetical (717n.).

S

715 **ingenti Sila summove Taburno**: ablatives of place where. Both locations are Italian: the Sila is a heavily forested plateau in Calabria, and Taburnus is a mountain (part of the Apennine range) in Campania.

716–17 **conversis . . ./ frontibus**: not so much ablative absolute as ablative of means with **inimica in proelia . . ./. . . incurrunt**; bulls use their foreheads to fight (721). **inimica in proelia: inimica** at first sight looks redundant as an epithet of **proelia**, but Virgil may use it to distinguish this bitter contest between the bulls from play-fighting or unserious skirmishing.

717 **magistri**: 'herd-masters', who look after cattle in the wild landscape; the fact that even these experienced figures withdraw emphasizes the fearsome nature of the bulls. **cessere**: 12n. The perfect amid the present tenses may explain why no human is intervening (for the herd-masters 'have withdrawn' already), in which case the clause should be seen as effectively a parenthesis (715–19n.); alternatively, it could be perfect of 'instantaneous action' (the herd-masters 'suddenly withdraw').

718 **metu**: ablative of cause, explaining **mutum**. **iuvencae**: the heifers have a personal interest in the questions of 719, since the dominant bull is likely to father their calves.

719 **quis nemori imperitet, quem tota armenta sequantur**: indirect questions after **mussant** (718); cf. 657–8. **nemori**: the locations specified in line 715 are both wooded, in places very densely. **armenta**: probably plural for singular; a true plural would add a grandeur to the scene, but bulls do not usually exhibit imperial ambitions.

720 **inter sese . . . vulnera miscent**: 'they exchange wounds with each other'. **sese**: 53n. **multa vi**: ablative of manner.

721 **cornuaque obnixi infigunt** clarify how the wounds are inflicted; **obnixi** is nominative masculine plural perfect participle from the deponent *obnitor*, agreeing with **illi** (720). **sanguine largo**: ablative of means, with **lavant** (722).

722   **gemitu**: ablative after **remugit** ('re-echoes with their groaning'). **nemus**: 719n.

723   **Daunius heros**: 22n.

724   **clipeis**: instrumental ablative, with **concurrunt** (712n.). **ingens fragor**: produced by the clash of shield on shield (cf. 712). **aethera**: accusative singular (this is a Greek accusative ending: the word *aether* is borrowed from Greek).

725–7   Virgil now turns to the grandest and most important spectator of all (cf. 704–9) – Jupiter, the king of the gods. In the *Aeneid*, Jupiter knows what is destined to happen in the future and is concerned to ensure that mortals and immortals do not interfere with the course of destiny. Here he weighs the fates of Aeneas and Turnus in a balance – apparently to display in advance the outcome of their single combat. The action does not seem to be witnessed by the human actors in Latium, and Jupiter may do this to warn other gods of the futility of interference. Cf. p. 19.

725–6   Jupiter holds up the scales, once the balance is level (**aequato examine** is ablative absolute); he then puts the fates of Aeneas and Turnus (the **duorum** of 726) in place, one in each scale-pan.

727   **quem damnet labor et quo vergat pondere letum**: indirect questions. The train of thought from 725–6 to 727 is elliptical, and a further clause needs to be supplied in translation: Jupiter 'placed the fates of the two men' in the scale-pans *in order to show* (or perhaps *see*) 'whom the struggle doomed and in what direction death sank down with its weight'. Virgil leaves the questions unanswered here (although it is clear from an early stage in the epic that Aeneas is destined to be victorious in the war).

728–952

The single combat between Aeneas and Turnus is narrated in two passages (710–90 and 887–952); the intervening lines show Jupiter acting to secure the outcome he desires (791–886). On the structure of the single combat, see pp. 16–17.

728–41

Turnus attempts to strike a decisive blow, but his sword-blade shatters on contact with Aeneas' armour.

728 impune putans: elliptical (for something like *putans id impune futurum esse*); tr. 'thinking it would go unpunished'. Turnus seems to think that the blow he will deliver in line 730 will be one to which Aeneas will not be able to respond.

728–9 consurgit . . . in ensem expresses Turnus' attempt to shift his body weight upwards so as to generate as much force as possible when he brings his sword down onto Aeneas. **corpore toto**: ablative of means, developing **consurgit. alte** is to be taken with **sublatum**.

730 Troes trepidique Latini: cf. 704–7 (and 699n.).

731 arrectaeque amborum acies: understand *sunt*. **amborum** refers to the two groups identified in line 730.

732 frangitur in medioque ardentem deserit ictu: understand *Turnum* or *eum* with **ardentem**. *-que* can be postponed (like *et*: 30n.) from its expected position; this sometimes happens to avoid *-que* following a monosyllabic preposition, as here.

733 ni fuga subsidio subeat: this is the protasis of a condition, from which the apodosis is missing and needs to be supplied from the sense of 732 (Turnus' sword broke [and this would have left him helpless and doomed], 'had not flight come to his aid'). **subeat**: present subjunctive, a vivid replacement for the expected pluperfect. **subsidio**: predicative dative. **Euro**: ablative of comparison, after **ocior** (adjective used adverbially).

734   capulum ignotum: explained in lines 735–41.

735   fama est ('it is said (that . . .)') introduces an indirect statement, with accusative **praecipitem** (understand *Turnum*) and infinitive **rapuisse** (737).

735-6   cum prima in proelia iunctos/ conscendebat equos seem to refer to a moment earlier in Book XII, when Turnus leaps onto his chariot to join battle after seeing Aeneas retreat, wounded (324–7: see p. 12). His excited haste on that occasion (324: cf. 735 **praecipitem**, 737 **dum trepidat**) makes it plausible that – as we learn only in 736–7 – he seized the wrong sword. **prima in proelia**: 103–4n.

736   patrio mucrone: cf. 89–91 (with 89–90n.).

737   ferrum: 16n. **aurigae . . . Metisci**: Metiscus is Turnus' charioteer; apart from this reference to his sword, he is only mentioned in the *Aeneid* when Juturna assumes his appearance and his role on the battlefield (623–4n.).

738-9   idque diu, dum terga dabant palantia Teucri,/ suffecit: the phase of the battle here indicated is narrated in lines 324–616. **id** refers to **ferrum** (737).

739   suffecit; postquam: adversative asyndeton (663–4n.). **arma dei . . . Volcania**: a grand expression (**Volcania** is more elevated in style than a simple genitive *Volcani*) to describe Aeneas' grand armour, which was forged for him by Vulcan (90–1n.) at Venus' request (VIII.370–453, 608–731). **ventum est**: impersonal passive.

740   **mortalis mucro**: Metiscus' sword-blade is not of divine origin, unlike the armour of Aeneas (739n.) and the sword of Daunus which Turnus should have been wielding (90–1n.).

740   **ictu**: ablative of cause (explaining **dissiluit** 741), or conceivably of place where ('in the blow') or more loosely of circumstance ('with the blow').

741   **fulva ... harena**: ablative of place where.

742–65

The first phase of the single combat is over; the second phase begins, as the unarmed Turnus flees from Aeneas. See pp. 16–17.

742   **ergo**: Turnus flees because he is (temporarily) without a weapon. **diversa ... aequora**: thus far, the setting for the battle of Book XII has been a single large plain (614n.), perhaps with identifiable sub-divisions (710n.); here we seem to glimpse distant or at least different plains, beyond this one: Turnus heads towards them, but his path will soon be blocked (743–5). **fuga**: ablative of means with **petit**.

743   **incertos implicat orbes**: lit. 'he entwines uncertain circles'; tr. 'he ran in criss-crossing uncertain circles'.

744   **enim**: 744–5 explain why Turnus was forced to run in circles (743), rather than escaping beyond the plain (which appears to have been his aim: 742). **densa ... corona**: ablative of means, with **inclusere**. **inclusere**: 12n. Understand *Turnum* or *eum* as object of this verb (and of **cingunt** in 745).

745   **vasta palus ... ardua moenia**: Virgil has not previously mentioned marshes in the vicinity of Latinus' city (to which the

moenia here belong), but the coastal zones of Latium did contain much marshy ground in antiquity.

746   nec minus takes its colour from the context in which it appears; here, 'and no less [vigorously] did Aeneas . . .'.

746–7   tardata sagitta/. . . genua impediunt: understand *Aenean* or *eum* as object. **sagitta** is ablative of means, with **tardata**. Aeneas was wounded by an arrow at XII.311–23; he was subsequently healed by Venus, but here (cf. 762) the wound continues to inhibit his movement.

747   cursumque recusant: lit. 'and refuse running'; tr. 'and would not let him run'.

748   trepidique: understand *Turni* or *eius*. **pede**: ablative of means, with **urget**.

749–57   Aeneas' pursuit of Turnus is compared to a hunting dog's chasing-down of a stag. The primary point of comparison lies in how close Aeneas and the dog get to their quarry, but there are multiple further correspondences between narrative and simile.

749–51   The word order of these lines is complex, although their grammatical structure is straightforward enough. **venator . . . canis** is the subject; **cervum** is the object of **nactus** (deponent perfect participle, agreeing with **canis**) and also of **instat**; the accusative participle phrases **inclusum . . . flumine** and **puniceae saeptum formidine pennae** indicate alternative situations in which the stag finds itself cornered.

750   puniceae saeptum formidine pennae: a *formido* ('scare') was a cord (with white and scarlet feathers attached) which was stretched around woodland where hunting was taking place; animals attempting to escape would be frightened back into the wood by the bright colours. **puniceae ... pennae** (genitive of the material of which the 'scare' consists) is singular for plural.

751   venator: noun used as adjective ('hunting'). **cursu ... et latratibus**: ablatives of means, with **instat**.

752   ille: the stag. **insidiis et ripa territus alta**: **insidiis** seems to refer to the *formido* (750), and **ripa ... alta** develops the scene outlined in **inclusum ... flumine** (749); **et** suggests that what were alternative situations (750 **aut**: 749–51n.) now both confront the stag.

753   mille fugit refugitque vias: intransitive verbs of motion can take an accusative object which indicates the extent of space traversed. **Umber**: usually an adjective, but here used as a noun to denote a well-known breed of hunting dog. Umbria was a district of north-central Italy, stretching from Etruria to the Adriatic Sea.

754   haeret ... iam iamque tenet: understand *cervum* or *eum* as the object of both verbs. **iam iamque** indicates that something seems to be imminent; tr. 'is just about to get hold [of the stag]'. **similisque tenenti**: lit. 'and like one that is getting hold'; tr. 'and looking like he is actually getting hold'.

755   increpuit ... elusus est: true perfect tenses ('has snapped ... has been mocked'). **malis**: ablative of instrument, with **increpuit**. **morsu ... inani**: looser ablative of means, with **elusus est** ('mocked by an empty bite').

756–7   These lines should probably be taken as part of the simile, rather than – as some have preferred – the resumption of the narrative.

756   clamor: if we remain in the scenario supposed by the simile, this most likely refers to noise made by the dog; but given that the presence of human hunters is implied by the *formido* (750n.), it is conceivable that the shouting may come from them.

A
Level

757   tumultu: ablative of means or cause, with **tonat**.

758   ille: Turnus. **simul fugiens ... simul increpat**: the second **simul** here is redundant in terms of sense, but serves to emphasize that Turnus continues to flee as he snaps at his men.

759   notumque efflagitat ensem: Turnus wants the sword he knows – the one which belonged to his father (89–91, 736); contrast **capulum ignotum** in 734.

760   contra: adverb ('in response').

761   si quisquam adeat: understand *ad Turnum*; **si quisquam** is stronger than *si quis*: 'if anyone whatsoever should go to [him]'. **terretque trementes**: the understood object of **terret** is *Rutulos* (cf. 758); **trementes** may indicate that they are already trembling (as a result of the personal threats in 760–1) when Aeneas terrifies them further – or it may be proleptic (94n.), indicating the physical result produced by the even greater threat in 762.

762   excisurum urbem minitans: understand *se* and *esse* (654–5n.). **saucius**: 746–7n.

763–4   Turnus seems to be running in large circles (cf. 743), then evading Aeneas and running along the same paths in the opposite direction.

763   totidemque retexunt: with **totidem**, understand *orbes* from the previous clause (*apo koinou*: 32–3n.).

764–5   neque ... levia aut ludicra petuntur/ praemia: *praemia ludicra* are prizes won at games (*ludi*); these and other trivial (**levia**) prizes are insignificant when set alongside the prize of a man's life (765).

766–90

The second phase of the single combat (742–65n.) has reached something of a stalemate. Aeneas clearly has the upper hand, since Turnus is without a weapon; yet the Trojan is unable to catch his adversary and himself lacks a missile weapon. This episode re-establishes both warriors' ability to fight, as Turnus regains his sword (but not his spear, which will force him to look elsewhere for a projectile later: 896–914n.) and Aeneas his spear. The divine help received by each warrior here adds drama to the passage, and reminds us of the stature of the two men and the significance of their duel.

766   sacer Fauno: trees sacred to divinities were a feature of Roman (and Greek) religion. Faunus was a god of the woodlands and of uncultivated countryside; moreover, he is in the *Aeneid* closely linked to Latium, as the father (and adviser: 27–8n.) of King Latinus. **foliis . . . amaris**: ablative of description, with **oleaster**.

767   hic: the area where Turnus is hemmed in, trying to flee from Aeneas. **venerabile lignum**: nominative, in apposition to **oleaster** (766). **nautis**: dative of the person judging, with **venerabile** ('worthy of reverence in the eyes of sailors').

768–9   The tree had been a site where sailors who had reached land safely would hang up clothes which they had vowed to the god in moments of danger at sea.

768   servati: the participle refers to *nautae*, who are easily understood from 767 as the subject of **solebant**.

768–9   figere dona . . ./. . . et votas suspendere vestes: 'theme and variation' (617–19n.), unless the **dona** are distinct from the **vestes** themselves.

769   Laurenti: 24n.

A
Level

770–1   The Trojans have cut down the tree (leaving a stump: 770n.) when clearing space for fighting to take place (771). This tree-clearance must have taken place within the last day or so (the Trojan forces only reached Latinus' city late the previous afternoon); it was perhaps done at the time the Trojans pitched camp during the previous evening (XI.915).

770   **stirpem** must in this line (unusually) denote the 'trunk' of the tree, removed by the Trojans; it cannot here mean 'stump', since that part of the tree remains in place (781). **nullo discrimine**: 'with no distinction [made]' (between this sacred tree and any other).

772   **hic ... huc ...**: both adverbs refer to the tree stump. **hasta Aeneae**: 711n.

772–3   **impetus** is subject and **illam** object of both **detulerat** and **tenebat**. The force (**impetus**) of the spear-cast has carried the spear down (**illam/ detulerat**) deep into the stump of the tree. **fixam**: either proleptic (94n.) after **detulerat**, or object of **tenebat** (with **et** postponed: 30n.). **lenta radice tenebat**: 'was holding [it] fast in the clinging root'.

774   **manu**: ablative of instrument, with **convellere**.

775–6   **teloque sequi quem prendere cursu/ non poterat**: **sequi** is governed by **voluit** (774); understand *Turnum* or *eum* as its object (and the antecedent of **quem**). **telo**: ablative of means, with **sequi** ('catch'). *telum* can refer to any weapon (*OLD* 3), but is typically applied to missile weapons and especially spears (as here: *OLD* 1). **cursu**: ablative of means (with **prendere**), balancing **telo**.

776   **formidine**: ablative of cause, with **amens**. Turnus is terrified that Aeneas might regain his spear while he remains unarmed; subsequent events (919–27) show that he is right to fear Aeneas' spear.

A
Level

777   **precor**: parenthetical (cf. 72–3n.). **miserere**: 43n.; the context makes it clear that Turnus is asking for pity for himself. **optima**: 'most kindly'.

778   **Terra**: Turnus prays to the Earth as a goddess; since she personifies the productive power of the ground, she can be thought likely to be angered by the Trojans' destruction of the wild olive growing in the soil. An Earth goddess (named *Tellus* or later *Terra*) was worshipped at Rome from an early period. **colui vestros si semper honores**: the ancient worshipper typically reminds divinities to whom he is praying of his services to them in the past (often, as here, employing a modest conditional clause), in the hope of some reciprocal favour – the so-called '*do ut des*' principle. **colui vestros . . . honores**: 'if I have carried out acts which bestow honour upon you' (presumably, acts of sacrifice).

779   **quos . . . Aeneadae . . . fecere profanos**: the antecedent of **quos** is strictly **honores** in 778; *profanus* is a technical term of Roman religion which means 'not sacred'. Turnus says that by cutting down the tree, the Trojans have removed the religious value from his acts of honour. **Aeneadae**: 12n. **bello**: ablative of means, with **fecere**. Insofar as the tree-clearance was deliberately undertaken to facilitate fighting on the spot (771), the Trojans can be said to have deprived the **honores** of sanctity 'by war'. **fecere**: 12n.

780   **opemque dei non cassa in vota vocavit**: lit. 'he called out for the assistance of the god to make his prayers not fruitless'. *in* followed by the accusative can be used to express purpose.

781   **lentoque in stirpe moratus**: *moror in* followed by the ablative means 'I delay over'. **stirpe** means 'stump' in this line (770n.).

782   **viribus . . . ullis**: ablative of means, with **discludere**.

782   morsus: plural for singular, unless the plural implies that the wood gripped the spear at multiple points.

783   acer: adjective used adverbially.

784–5   Turnus' sister Juturna (623–30n.) last appeared in the narrative at 682–3, left behind as Turnus went to fight Aeneas. Here she re-adopts her disguise as Turnus' charioteer Metiscus (623–4n.) to intervene in events once more.

784   mutata: middle-passive (623–4n.), 'having changed herself'.

785   ensem: presumably, the sword which had belonged to Daunus (759n.).

786–7   Aeneas' mother Venus gives him practical help at various points throughout the *Aeneid*, including on two occasions earlier in Book XII (see p. 12). This is her final appearance in the epic.

786   quod: connecting relative (= *et id*); the neuter relative pronoun can refer back to the whole action of a previous clause or sentence, rather than to a specific noun or pronoun: so, here it refers to Turnus being given the sword by Juturna. **quod Venus audaci nymphae indignata licere**: **indignata** is perfect deponent participle (agreeing with **Venus**), followed by accusative (**quod** = *et id*) and infinitive (**licere**). *licet* is usually an impersonal verb, but with a neuter pronoun as subject can mean '(something) is permitted' (*OLD* 3); the person to whom something is permitted appears in the dative. Lit. 'and Venus, indignant that this was permitted to the bold nymph'; tr. 'and Venus, indignant that the bold nymph was permitted to do this'. **nymphae**: 885–6n.

787   telumque: 775–6n.

788–90   The two warriors stand facing each other, weapons and courage restored; 788–9 use the 'theme and variation' technique

A Level

(617–19n.) to emphasize this point. 790 leaves us with a memorable tableau, before our attention is temporarily redirected elsewhere.

788 **olli**: an archaic form of *illi* (here nominative plural: contrast 18n.). **sublimes**: either 'imposingly tall' or 'high-spirited'; both senses may be in play. **armis**: ablative of means, if **sublimes** is physical; ablative of cause, if **sublimes** is psychological. The noun refers to the weapons which the warriors have recently recovered (785–7). **animisque**: ablative of respect, with **refecti**.

789 **hic ... hic ...**: 'this one ... that one ...' (Turnus and Aeneas respectively). **hasta**: ablative of means, with **arduus** (and perhaps **acer**).

790 **adsistunt**: 'they took up their positions'. **contra certamina Martis** seems to mean 'facing the contests of Mars'; **Martis** may be metonymy for 'war' or 'battle' (1n., 712n.), but the suggestion that the struggle awaiting Aeneas and Turnus somehow belongs to the war god gives this line a grim grandeur (cf. 73). **anheli** is probably genitive singular, agreeing with **Martis** (Mars, or battle, is 'breathless' in the sense that violent struggle causes breathlessness); but it could be masculine nominative plural, referring to Aeneas and Turnus (who are plausibly 'out of breath' after running and fighting).

791–842

With Aeneas and Turnus poised to recommence combat, Virgil now abruptly switches the focus of the narrative to the divinities Jupiter and Juno, who are watching the fighting as they were earlier in Book XII (134–7, 725–7). The scene is presented almost exclusively in direct speech. Juno's words show that she remains hostile towards the Trojan race (811–12, 828) and supportive of the Italian peoples (819–28); but

A Level

the conversation sees Jupiter successfully detach his wife and sister from practical assistance to Turnus and from her obstruction of destiny (cf. 843–86n.). In this sense, the scene brings to an end (cf. **finis** 793) Juno's activity as chief adversary of the Trojans within the poem, and brings resolution to the conflict between the wills of Jupiter and Juno which has lain behind much of the action of the *Aeneid*. The three speeches also allow Virgil to open up the temporal perspective of the poem, looking ahead to the relatively near future – the apotheosis of Aeneas (794–5n.), the development of the mixed Trojan–Latin community (821–5, 834–7) – but also to the more distant future, in the announcement of the nature of the Roman people (838–40, cf. 827) which will ultimately spring from that Trojan-Latin community.

791   Iunonem: Juno has been consistently hostile to the Trojans throughout the *Aeneid*. The reasons for her angry hatred of Aeneas and his people are explained at the beginning of the epic (I.12–32). She helped the Greeks to destroy Troy, and has persecuted the refugees both on their journey and in Italy. **rex omnipotentis Olympi:** Olympus is located by ancient authors sometimes on the mountain of the same name in northern Greece, and sometimes in the sky. It is suitably *omnipotens* as the abode of the most powerful gods, and especially of Jupiter.

792   fulva . . . de nube: clouds offer a convenient vantage-point from which gods (on them, or in them) can observe events in the human world at relatively close quarters. For this cloud, cf. 796, 810, 842. **pugnas . . . tuentem:** gods are often shown watching the fighting in the second half of the *Aeneid* (as in most ancient martial epic).

793–806   Jupiter accuses Juno of being behind Juturna's interventions in support of Turnus, and forbids any further interference.

793   quae iam finis erit: the question is phrased in very general terms; but the remainder of the speech, and its context within the surrounding narrative and the whole poem, make it clear that Jupiter is asking about the 'end' of Juno's persecution of the Trojans (cf. 797, 803–5) and of her support for their opponents (cf. 798–9). **quid denique restat?**: **quid** is again unspecific, but the rest of the speech (cf. 803–6) makes it clear that Jupiter is asking what course of action is left for Juno to attempt.

794–6 Juno cannot prevent Aeneas becoming a god. So, why is she behaving as she is?

794–5 **indigetem Aenean scis . . ./ deberi caelo**: **indigetem** is a predicate; 'you know Aeneas is destined for heaven as an *Indiges*'. The *Indigetes* are a category of Roman divinity about whose origin and nature we are ill-informed. Judging from the fact that Aeneas will become one – and from other evidence – it is possible that they were understood as mortal men who had become gods. Aeneas' status as *Indiges* is attested in other ancient texts and by archaeology.

794 **et scire fateris**: understand *te* as the object of **fateris**.

795 **fatisque ad sidera tolli**: the construction depends on **Aenean scis** in 794. **fatis**: 'by fate' (that is, in accordance with fate: *OLD* 5). **sidera**: the stars of the sky, where Aeneas' home will be (791n.) when he is a god. **tolli**: the present tense implies that the process of Aeneas' deification is effectively already underway.

796 **qua spe**: so-called 'comitative' ablative ('with what hope . . .?').

797 **mortalin** = *mortaline* (cf. 874). **violari . . . divum**: accusative and infinitive after **decuit**. **mortalin . . . vulnere**: ablative of means, with **violari**. Jupiter refers to the wounding of Aeneas by an arrow earlier in the Book (746–7n.). **divum** again (795n.) presents Aeneas as effectively already a god.

798–9 **aut ensem . . ./ ereptum reddi Turno et vim crescere victis?**: two accusatives and infinitives (**ensem . . ./ . . . reddi** and **vim**

crescere), depending on **decuit** in 797. Jupiter refers to very recent events (784–5, 788–90).

798   (quid enim sine te Iuturna valeret?): **enim** explains why Jupiter is blaming Juno for events brought about by the intervention of Juturna. **quid** is internal accusative (843n.) with **valeret** (potential subjunctive): 'what power would Juturna have?'. Juno later acknowledges a partial validity in Jupiter's claim here (813–17n.).

799   ereptum presumably refers to a hurried snatching-up of Turnus' sword by Juturna before she gave it to him (785). **victis**: dative of 'personal interest'; the plural surprises, though perhaps Turnus is seen as standing for all the Latin forces.

800   desine looks general, but its specific application is clear from the context (793n.). **precibus ... nostris**: ablative of means. **inflectere**: 43n.

801   ne te tantus edit tacitam dolor: purpose. clause; **edit** is an archaic form of the present subjunctive (the classical form is *edat*).

801–2   ne ... et mihi curae/ saepe tuo dulci tristes ex ore recursent: 'and so that bitter anxieties do not keep coming back to me [so] often from your sweet lips'. **mihi** is dative after *recurso* or of personal interest.

803   ventum ... est: impersonal passive (cf. 739).

803–5 Jupiter lists some of the miseries Juno has inflicted on the Trojans and the Italians during the course of the poem, before banning her from further intervention. The four infinitives all depend on **potuisti**.

803–4   terris agitare vel undis/ Troianos potuisti: **terris** and **undis** are ablatives of place where. This summarizes the whole poem. Juno has hounded the Trojans on land in the Trojan War and more recently in Latium (804n.); she roused the storm at sea which drove the Trojans off course at the beginning of the epic (I.34–80).

804   infandum accendere bellum: the war between the Trojans and the Latins, which Juno 'inflamed' at VII.286–640 (pp. 8–9).

805   deformare domum et luctu miscere hymenaeos: the two infinitive-phrases describe related situations, and **luctu** (ablative of means) can be taken with the first as well as the second. 'To disfigure the household with grief' refers primarily to the effect of the suicide of queen Amata upon the royal household in Latium (XII.604–21); that suicide was, at least in part, a product of Juno's activity earlier in the poem (VII.341–405). 'To throw a marriage into confusion with grief' refers to the impact of Juno's behaviour (in starting the war and interfering with Amata) on the proposed marriage of Aeneas and Lavinia (29–31n.). Juno was the Roman goddess of marriage, so there is some element of perversion in this action.

806   ulterius temptare veto: understand *te* as object of **veto**. **ulterius** is the neuter accusative singular of the comparative adjective *ulterior* (for which no positive form exists); here it is used as a substantive: 'I forbid [you] to attempt anything further.' **orsus**: understand *est*.

807   dea . . . Saturnia: the god Saturn was considered (as a result of assimilation to the Greek Titan Kronos) the father of Jupiter and Juno (830n.). **summisso . . . vultu**: ablative of description. **contra**: 'in reply'; this useful adverb allows Virgil to dispense with a verb of speaking (which should be added in translation).

808–28   Juno insists that she knew Jupiter's will already, and has accordingly withdrawn. She yields to Jupiter's demands, but makes a solemn request of her own.

808   ista . . . quia nota mihi tua . . . voluntas: understand *est*. The 'will' of Jupiter to which Juno refers is that expressed throughout the

A
Level

speech he has just given, and summarized in his final three words
(806) – that Juno should not interfere any further in events in Latium.

809   invita: adjective used adverbially.

810–12   The construction is elliptical: these lines contain the
apodosis of a condition, for which the implied protasis is 'if I did not
know your will'; this can be conveyed in English simply by supplying
the word 'otherwise' at the beginning of 810.

810–11 Accusative (**me . . . solam**) and infinitive (**pati**) after **videres**.

810   aeria . . . sede: ablative of place where; Juno is referring to her
cloud (792n.).

811   digna indigna: neuter accusative plural objects of **pati**. The
compressed phrase literally means 'to suffer all things without regard
to the question whether they are suitable or unsuitable to be suffered'
– which amounts to 'to suffer all kinds of things'.

811–12   flammis cincta . . ./ starem: 'I would be standing there,
surrounded (**cincta** feminine nominative singular) by flames.' The
flames envisaged by Juno seem to belong to her and to represent her
terrifying power (rather than being the flames of Latinus' city: 656n.,
672–3n.).

812   inimica in proelia: the epithet is hardly necessary (716–17n.),
but does here emphasize the hostility that Juno still clearly feels
towards the Trojans.

813–17   Juno acknowledges that she did earlier in the day prompt
Juturna to intervene to help Turnus (cf. XII.138–60) – but solemnly
denies that she authorized the shooting of Aeneas.

814   pro vita maiora audere probavi: understand *Iuturnam* from
the previous clause (*apo koinou*: 32–3n.) as the object of **probavi**. Tr.

'I authorized Juturna to dare to undertake greater things (i.e. greater than she otherwise would have done) for the sake of his life.'

815 non ut tela tamen, non ut contenderet arcum: contenderet is to be understood (*apo koinou*: 32–3n.) with the first *ut*-clause as well as the second. These are restrictive consecutive clauses; having admitted in 813–14 that she did prompt Juturna to intervene, Juno now qualifies that admission by saying she carried out this prompting 'not however [to the point] that she (Juturna) should shoot arrows (**tela**: cf. 775–6n.), not [to the point] that she should draw a bow'. Juno is here responding to Jupiter's indignant question in 797.

816 Stygii caput implacabile fontis: 'the implacable source of the spring-water of the Styx'. The Styx is the most famous of the rivers of the underworld; it is **implacabile** as not pardoning any false oath sworn by it (817n.).

817 una superstitio superis quae reddita divis: a relative clause of some difficulty. The antecedent is not an individual word, but the whole action of the previous line – that is, the swearing of an oath by the Styx; understood as a 'thing', this action as antecedent would usually require the neuter relative *quod*: but here the relative pronoun is attracted into the feminine (**quae**) gender of the predicate **una superstitio**. Tr. 'which has been allotted (with **reddita**, understand *est*) to the gods above as the only object of our religious awe'. The gods swear by the Styx already in Homer; its deep association with death seems to be what inspires awe and dread in the immortals.

818 A momentous development in the *Aeneid*, given a line all to itself: the chief antagonist of Aeneas and the Trojans finally gives way. **pugnasque**: object of both **exosa** and **relinquo**.

819–28 Having yielded to Jupiter's demand, Juno now makes a solemn (819–20) request. Looking forward beyond the end of the

poem (821–2), she begs that the people of Latium should not be
regarded as Trojan (823–5) – rather, they and their descendants
should be considered Italian (826–7). She urges Jupiter to recognize
that Troy has perished and is no more (828). Juno knows that the
future of the new, mixed race is foreordained, and splendid: in these
lines, she seeks to affect not what will happen hereafter, but instead
how that future will be regarded.

819–20 Given that this request immediately follows the line in
which Juno announces that she is yielding, the asyndeton at the
beginning of 819 should be regarded as adversative (663–4n.). **illud te
. . ./. . . obtestor**: the verb here takes two accusative objects. **illud**: 'this
particular thing' (*OLD* 12); the word looks forward to the requests of
821–8. **nulla fati quod lege tenetur**: 'which is not bound by any law of
fate'; Juno's requests in 821–8 can be accommodated within the wider
framework of destiny. **pro maiestate tuorum**: 'for the sake of the
grandeur of your people (653n.)'. The people of Latium (who will be
the focus of Juno's requests in 821–8) can be regarded
as related to Jupiter through his father Saturn, who was their king
Latinus' great-grandfather (cf. VII.47–9).

821–2 **cum . . ./ component, cum . . . iungent**: the subject of each
verb seems to be both the people of Latium and the Trojans, although
the former are uppermost in Juno's mind in 819–20 and 823–7.

821 **cum iam**: 'at that time when'. **conubiis . . . felicibus**: ablative of
means, with **pacem . . ./ component**; the marriage will be the means
by which the people of Latium and the Trojans arrange a settled peace.
The marriage to which Juno refers is that of Aeneas to Latinus'
daughter Lavinia, which was arranged in Book VII but derailed by
Juno herself (29–31n., 805n.). **(esto)**: third-person singular imperative
of *sum*, typically used to mean 'so be it!' when a speaker concedes a
situation; Juno's tone may be a little more generous ('may it be so').

**A
Level**

The word goes closely with **felicibus**: the goddess of marriage (805n.) gives her reluctant blessing to the union, accepting that it will be 'successful' or 'well-omened'.

822   leges et foedera iungent: 'they will make laws and agreements to bind them together'.

823–5   A prohibition, with **ne ...**/ **neu ... iubeas** followed by accusative **indigenas ... Latinos** and three infinitives (**mutare, fieri** and **vocari**) in 823–4 and then by another accusative **viros** and two infinitives **mutare** and **vertere** in 825.

823–4   vetus ... nomen mutare .../... Troas fieri ... Teucrosque vocari: Juno begs that the people of Latium should not become or even be called Trojan. The first and third phrases here express the same idea in different ways, and this is arguably true of the second phrase, too: 'theme and variation' (617–19n.) gives emphasis to the goddess' most crucial request. **vetus ... nomen**: it is implied that the people of this area have always been called *Latini*.

825   aut vocem mutare viros aut vertere vestem: on the construction, see 823–5n. Juno restates the object of **iubeas** with **viros** here (these men are the same as the **indigenas ... Latinos** of 823–4), probably to emphasize that changing language or altering their clothing could undermine their masculinity. At times in the *Aeneid*, the Trojans' appearance and, indeed, nature is regarded as unmanly by their opponents (98–9n., 99–100n.).

826–7   Juno presents her positive requests (819–28n.) with three jussive subjunctives in an ascending tricolon; the emphasis in each clause is on the proper names.

826   sit Latium: 'let Latium exist' (that is, Latium as it is, without changes to its name or nature: cf. 823–4), or 'let the land be Latium'. **sint Albani per saecula reges**: 'let the kings throughout the ages be

Alban'. Alba Longa was a settlement in Latium, of special significance for the Romans as the home of Romulus' mother and ancestors. In the *Aeneid*, Jupiter prophesies at I.267–74 its foundation by Aeneas' son Ascanius, and subsequent rule by kings of Trojan blood; but in the underworld at VI.760–76, Aeneas' father Anchises presents him with a vision of the future, in which Alba Longa will be ruled by kings descended from a son Silvius whom Lavinia will bear to Aeneas. These seem to be alternative versions of the early history of Alba; certainly, they are difficult to reconcile. At any rate, Juno here requests that although the kings of this settlement will be of mixed Italian and Trojan heritage, they should be in essence and in name Alban (and therefore Italian, or at least certainly not Trojan).

827   sit Romana potens Itala virtute propago: 'let the race be Roman, mighty with an Italian courage'. Juno asks that the descendants of the mixed Latin and Trojan people be Roman, and that the predominant element in their character be derived from their Italian heritage; again, the point is 'Roman and Italian – not Trojan.'

828   occidit, occideritque sinas ... Troia: **Troia** is the subject of both **occidit** (a true perfect: 'Troy has fallen') and **occiderit**, which is perfect subjunctive after the jussive subjunctive **sinas** (lit. 'allow that it has fallen': that is, 'allow it to remain fallen'); *sino* can be followed by a subjunctive without *ut*, as here (*OLD* 6b). **cum nomine**: 'along with its name'; much of lines 823–7 has been directed at ensuring that the name of Troy will die out as completely as the city itself has perished.

829   olli: 18n.; the dative depends on **subridens. hominum rerumque repertor**: Jupiter.

830–40   Jupiter gives assent to Juno's wishes for the people of Latium; he adds that he will introduce their religion, and that she will be greatly honoured by them.

A
Level

830–1 Juno's anger (towards the Trojans, as demonstrated throughout the speech she has just given and throughout the poem) is taken to prove that she is truly Jupiter's sister and Saturn's daughter. Saturn had castrated his own father, and later swallowed his own children (the five born before Jupiter); Jupiter's anger is central to many familiar episodes of myth (for example, the punishment of Prometheus, or the Flood).

830 **Saturnique altera proles**: **altera** here means 'a second', 'another', rather than 'the second (of two)'. Jupiter and Juno were two of six children born to Saturn and Ops (the others being Vesta, Ceres, Pluto and Neptune); cf. 807n.

831 **irarum tantos volvis sub pectore fluctus**: this striking expression combines two senses of the verb *volvo*, which literally means 'I roll' but can also have the metaphorical sense 'I turn over in the mind'. **tantos . . . fluctus** is a natural object for the verb in the first sense, but not in the second; **irarum** (genitive of material, and plural for singular) and **sub pectore** ('inside (*OLD sub* 1c) your breast') are better suited to the second sense than the first.

833 Jupiter yields to Juno what she has asked; this significant moment in their reconciliation is expressed in simple language, and given a line to itself (cf. 818n.). **do quod vis**: understand *id* as the antecedent to **quod** (12n.); Jupiter expands on his offer in 834–7. **victusque volensque**: *-que . . . -que* here does mean 'both . . . and . . .' (23n.).

834 **Ausonii**: the name *Ausonia* is typically used in the *Aeneid* to denote the part of central Italy which lies south of the Apennine mountains; this area includes Latium. The name **Ausonii** can be applied to any (or all) of the various peoples who live in this area.

835 **utque est nomen erit**: **ut** is here used predicatively (*OLD* 14); 'and [their] name will be as it is [now]'.

A Level

835-6   commixti corpore tantum/ subsident Teucri: 'the Trojans, mingled [with the people of Latium] in body only, will sink into insignificance'. The precise image in **subsident** is elusive, but the verb can denote sinking within a liquid (*OLD* 4), something physical giving way or collapsing (*OLD* 5), or the fading of strong forces of nature (*OLD* 6). Jupiter tells Juno that the Trojans' only contribution to the new mixed culture will be to its bloodline – by intermarriage, or at least producing children, with the women of Latium (almost all the Trojans who have come to Italy are men: the female refugees were mostly left behind on Sicily in Book V).

837   faciamque omnes uno ore Latinos: **omnes** (which seems to refer to all the people who will be part of the new mixed community, both those of Italian heritage and those of Trojan heritage) is the object of **faciam**, and **Latinos** a predicate adjective. **uno ore** is ablative of description. Tr. 'I will make them all people of Latium, with one language.'

838-9   videbis is the main verb, followed by accusative (**genus**) and infinitive (**ire**).

838   The line consists of **genus** along with the relative clause of which it is the antecedent: more straightforwardly arranged, *genus quod mixtum sanguine Ausonio hinc surget* ('the race which, after it has been mixed with Ausonian blood, will rise up from this origin'). **hinc**: that is, from (unpromising, as Juno might think) Trojan origins. **Ausonio**: 834n.

839   pietate: ablative of respect. *Pietas* is the quality of dutifulness: for human beings, this meant, above all, doing one's duty to the gods, but also one's duty to one's country, to one's family and to other dependants. Jupiter says that the race which will rise from the union of Trojan and Italian blood will go beyond all other men in displaying this virtue, and even beyond the gods (a striking claim, although it is true that Greco-Roman divinities do not always exhibit an especially strong sense of duty). Although Jupiter does not name the Romans, it will have been clear to ancient readers that he has that people in mind: *pietas* was emphasized by Roman thinkers as a quality in which their community excelled.

840   tuos aeque celebrabit honores: 'will perform ceremonies of honour for you to the same degree'. Juno was, indeed, a central figure in Roman religion, both as one of the 'Triad' (along with Jupiter and Minerva) worshipped on the Capitoline hill in the most important temple in Rome, and in her own right: temples were dedicated to her in various parts of the city, and she was worshipped at a number of festivals.

841   mentem ... retorsit: the image shows the effort required for Juno to perform the change of mind which Jupiter has asked of her.

842   caelo: ablative of place from which, without a preposition (the prefix of **excedit** does some of the work of a preposition). **nubemque relinquit**: 792n. This is the final action of Juno in the poem.

843–86

In detaching Juno from support for Turnus, Jupiter has succeeded in removing the most significant obstacle to Aeneas' victory and to the movement of destiny. He now turns his attention to Turnus' other divine helper, Juturna. This time, Jupiter does not interfere directly, in person, but employs an intermediary – the mysterious Dira. The Dira is sent initially as a sign to Juturna (834), and she succeeds in deterring the nymph from further activity (869–86); but the Dira also has a profound effect on Turnus himself (865–8n.). Thus, this scene prepares for the final movement of the poem (887–952), both by removing Juturna and by weakening Turnus' ability to resist Aeneas.

A
Level

843 genitor: Jupiter. **aliud . . . volutat**: **aliud** is internal accusative (where the word in the accusative – typically a neuter pronoun or adjective – is not an external object of the verb, but instead helps to define the action of that verb); 'turned over another thought'.

844 Iuturnamque . . . fratris dimittere ab armis: 'to dismiss Juturna from supporting her brother's fighting'. Juturna was last seen in the narrative giving Turnus his sword (784–5); **armis** here may refer specifically to such activity, but probably means 'military activity' more generally.

845 dicuntur geminae pestes: understand *esse. pestis* means 'destruction' or 'something which brings destruction', often 'plague'; **pestes** here perhaps 'bringers of destruction'. **geminae**: here 'twin' or 'two born at the same birth' (see 846–7). **cognomine Dirae**: 'named the Dirae'; *dirus* is a strong word, denoting something very ill-omened or terrifying (or both). The Latin name of these creatures is usually retained in English translation; it means something like 'the Dread ones'.

846–8 The Dirae are closely associated with (but not identical to) the Furies, three goddesses of vengeance (named Megaera, Tisiphone and Allecto: the latter plays a major role in *Aeneid* VII). The Furies are daughters of Night (in Virgil) and dwell in the underworld. The Dirae were born from the same mother, but differ from the Furies in dwelling on Olympus with Jupiter (849–50), and in acting not as ministers of vengeance but as harbingers of destruction (850n.). **quas . . . Nox . . ./. . . tulit . . . revinxit/. . . addidit**: **Nox** is the subject of all three verbs; **quas** (antecedent **Dirae** 845) is the object of the first two, but strictly **addidit** requires a dative object (so understand *quibus*).

846–7 quas et . . . Nox . . . Megaeram/ uno eodemque tulit partu: **partu** is ablative of means, with **tulit**; **et** follows on from **eodem**: 'whom Night bore in one and the same birth as (she bore) Megaera'.

846 **Tartaream ... Megaeram**: 14n., 846–8n. **Nox intempesta**: when applied to night as a time, **intempesta** usually means 'the dead of (night)', 'deepest (night)' (*OLD* 1); but it is not easy to see how this meaning of the adjective could be applied to the goddess Night, and an alternative meaning 'timeless' seems more suitable here.

847–8 **paribusque revinxit/ serpentum spiris**: object **quas** (846–8n.); **serpentum** is genitive plural (possessive, with **spiris**). **paribus**: Night girded the Dirae with snakes, just as she did Megaera (the Furies are typically portrayed with snakes for hair).

848 **ventosasque addidit alas**: understand *quibus* (846–8n.). The Dirae are winged, again like the Furies.

849 **hae**: the two Dirae. **saevi . . . regis**: Jupiter, who can be 'savage' in his punishments – as will soon be clear from his treatment of Turnus (853–918); cf. 830–1n.

850 **apparent**: the verb is used elsewhere of officials who attend upon Roman magistrates. The presence of the Dirae at Jupiter's court seems to be permanent. **acuuntque metum mortalibus aegris**: these words clarify the function of the Dirae, which is to inspire or deepen dread in afflicted mortals (**mortalibus aegris**: dative of personal interest). It seems from Virgil and from other Roman sources that, generally (but cf. 913–14n.), the Dirae do not themselves cause destruction; rather, they act as signs of its coming and, for that reason, they cause dread.

851–2 Virgil explains the circumstances in which the clause **acuuntque metum mortalibus aegris** applies: the Dirae are employed to generate fear whenever Jupiter is planning death, disease and (although see 852n.) war.

851 **deum**: genitive plural (78n.), with **rex**.

A
Level

852   meritas . . . bello territat urbes: bello could be ablative of means, with **territat**; but it may be ablative of cause, with **meritas** ('terrifies cities which have deserved punishment because of war' – presumably, that is, because they have fought wars unsanctioned by Jupiter).

853   harum: of the Dirae. **celerem:** adjective used adverbially.

854   inque omen Iuturnae occurrere iussit: the object of **iussit** is **unam** (853); Jupiter has ordered the Dira to rush to confront Juturna 'so as to be an omen' (**in**: 780n.).

855   celerique . . . turbine: ablative of manner, with **fertur.**

856–9   The flight of the Dira from Olympus to Latium is compared to that of an arrow. The simile illustrates the speed and the unexpected arrival of the Dira; the references to poison and to the Parthian bowman convey something of her menace.

856   nervo: ablative of source or means, with **impulsa.**

857–8   A relative clause: **quam** (antecedent **sagitta** 856) is the object of **torsit,** of which the subject is **Parthus** in 857 (subsequently expanded to **Parthus sive Cydon** in 858).

857   armatam describes the arrow (**quam**). **felle:** ablative of means, with **armatam. saevi . . . veneni:** either possessive or defining genitive, with **felle.** The use of poisoned arrows (typically using snake venom) is widely attested in antiquity. **Parthus:** the Parthians in Virgil's day controlled a large territory (most of which now lies within the modern countries Iraq and Iran), and constituted something like a rival superpower beyond the eastern borders of the Roman empire. Tension between the two empires spilled over into major military campaigns in the mid-first century BC, in which the Romans gained first-hand experience of the Parthians' brilliance as archers (notably in a catastrophic defeat at Carrhae in 53 BC).

A Level

858 **Cydon**: Cydonia was a city on the island of Crete; the island produced the most renowned archers in the ancient Mediterranean world. **telum immedicabile**: accusative, in apposition to **quam**; cf. 775–6n.

859 **stridens et . . . incognita**: both describe the **sagitta** (856). *strido* is favoured by Virgil to denote the sound made by weapons as they fly through the air: whirring, or whizzing (cf. 691). The arrow here is 'unrecognized' since it is flying through a dark cloud.

celeres . . . transilit umbras: the adjective **celeres** makes little sense with **umbras** ('darkness', referring to the **nubem** of 856); **celeres** must therefore be a transferred epithet. This artificial figure of speech involves the application of an adjective which clearly suits one noun in a clause to a different noun, which it does not suit; in this case, **celeres** is transferred from **sagitta** (856) to **umbras**. (In translation, the adjective must be transferred back to the noun it suits.) The transferred epithet is the most frequently found type of hypallage in the *Aeneid* (hypallage is a catch-all term, covering figures of speech which involve 'the transposition of the natural relations of two elements in a proposition' (*OED*): these are some of the most peculiar, and difficult, stylistic phenomena in ancient poetry).

860 **Nocte**: ablative of source, after **sata**; 'the daughter of Night'.

861 **acies videt Iliacas atque agmina Turni**: the disposition of the troops which greets the Dira as she arrives is that established in the narrative at 704–7.

862 **alitis ... parvae**: an owl, to judge from lines 863–4. **in ... subitam collecta figuram**: **subitam** is adjective used adverbially; its adverbial force should be applied to **collecta** (middle-passive: 623–4n.): 'having shrunk herself suddenly into the form'.

864 **nocte**: ablative of time when. **serum**: accusative of neuter adjective used adverbially (700n.), with **canit**. **importuna**: neuter accusative plural, internal accusative (843n.) after **canit**; 'sings late at night her ill-omened songs'.

865–8 The Dira was sent as a sign to Juturna (854, cf. 843–4); the creature performs her duty primarily by flying at Turnus. Her appearance and behaviour is clearly sufficient for Juturna to recognize the omen (869–86); the Dira also successfully unnerves Turnus (867–8, cf. 895), and, indeed, will have some practical influence on the outcome of his combat with Aeneas (913–14n.).

865 **versa**: middle-passive (623–4n.). **ora**: plural for singular.

865–6 **se . . ./ fertque refertque**: 'made her way again and again'; the first *-que* here need not be translated (23n.). **alis**: ablative of means, with **verberat**.

867 **illi**: Turnus; possessive dative (used especially with parts of the body: there is some overlap with the dative of personal interest), with **membra**. **formidine**: ablative of cause, explaining **torpor**.

868 **arrectaeque . . . comae**: understand *sunt*. **horrore**: ablative of cause. **faucibus**: ablative of place where, or dative after **haesit**.

869 **procul**: Juturna recognizes the Dira 'from a distance', by her sound. Virgil seems to be saying not that she hears the Dira coming from a long way off (for the creature's appearance is sudden: 862), but rather that Juturna is lurking a little way from Turnus when the Dira arrives, yet is still able to recognize the nature of the creature from there. **Dirae stridorem et alas**: probably hendiadys (41–2n.), 'the whirring of the Dira's wings'.

870–1 Juturna has immediately recognized the Dira (869). It is clear from these lines that she understands the significance of the creature's appearance, as a harbinger of Turnus' death; for she performs three gestures typical of female mourning in antiquity: loosening and rending of the hair (870), tearing of the face and beating of the breast (871).

871 **unguibus ora . . . foedans et pectora pugnis**: **foedans** with **ora** (plural for singular) implies the drawing of blood, with **pectora** (plural for singular) bruising or at least blotches. **unguibus** and **pugnis** are ablatives of instrument.

872–84 Juturna's final utterance in the poem is one of utter desolation. She recognizes that she must abandon Turnus (875–8); a series of despairing questions precedes (872–4) and follows (878–84) this acknowledgement. The speech is a monologue; it becomes clear at 918 that Turnus did not see his sister or hear her words at this point.

872 **quid**: here an internal accusative (843n.) after **iuvare**, meaning 'in what respect?' (*OLD quis* 15).

873 **quid . . . durae superat mihi**: seems to mean 'what is left for me, after I have endured this?'; but the usage of *durus* here to mean 'enduring' or 'suffering' (in a negative sense: contrast *OLD* 3) is unusual and hard to parallel.

873–4 **qua . . . arte**: ablative of means, with **morer** (deliberative subjunctive). **tibi**: dative of personal interest. **lucem**: 'life' (660n.).

874 **talin** = **taline** (cf. 797). **talin . . . monstro**: dative after **me opponere**.

875–8 Juturna is already leaving. There is no need for the Dira to intimidate her: she knows that the appearance of the Dira as an owl signifies death for Turnus, and that this is Jupiter's will.

875 **iam iam**: 676n. **ne me terrete timentem**: 72–3n.; either 'do not terrify me – I who am (already) afraid', or (with **timentem** proleptic: 94n.) 'do not terrify me so that I become afraid'.

A
Level

876   obscenae volucres: it is unclear why Juturna addresses the Dira here (and in **terrete** 875) using a plural. **alarum verbera**: cf. 866, 869.

877   letalemque sonum seems to refer to the owl's screeching (866); this is a 'sound of death', since it is taken as an omen of death.

878   magnanimi: bitterly sarcastic.

878–84   Juturna was given immortality as a water-nymph by Jupiter as 'compensation' after he had taken her virginity, apparently by rape (XII.139–41); she had been born mortal, like her brother. In the nymph's last lines in the poem, she laments that this immortality has become a curse.

878   haec pro virginitate reponit?: 'is he (Jupiter) giving me *this* in return for my virginity?' **haec** is neuter accusative plural, and refers to the whole situation in which Juturna now finds herself.

879–80   'Theme and variation' (617–19n.) in the two questions emphasizes Juturna's point.

879–80   mortis .../ condicio: 'the law of death' – that is, the condition imposed by nature upon human beings that they must die.

880–1 The construction is elliptical: we have the apodosis of a condition, for which the protasis implied (by the questions in 879–80) is 'if he had not made me immortal'; in translation, simply supplying 'otherwise' will convey this (810–12n.).

880   tantos finire dolores: presumably, by suicide.

881   misero fratri: dative of the person accompanied, after **comes ire**.

882–4   Juturna dwells upon the prospect of eternal life, in despair.

882   immortalis ego?: 'I, immortal?'. Juturna contemplates in the bluntest terms the horror of living forever (that is, without her brother – as the next sentence makes clear).

A
Level

882–3 aut quicquam mihi dulce meorum/... erit?: aut has mystified scholars here, and it is difficult to see how 'or' is a suitable introduction to this question. The subject of **erit** is **quicquam** (neuter nominative singular), upon which **meorum** (partitive genitive, neuter plural) depends; **dulce** is predicate, and **mihi** dative of person judging. The question seems to mean: 'will any part of my life (lit. any one of my things) be sweet for me?'.

883–4 o: makes a question more emotional (*OLD* 3b; cf. 19n.). **quae .../ terra** is the subject of **dehiscat** (potential subjunctive). **ima** describes **terra**, but also helps to explain **satis**: 'what lowest depth of earth could gape sufficiently (low) for me'.

884 Manesque deam demittat ad imos?: 'and let a goddess go down to the lowest depth of the underworld?'. The name of the Manes (646–7n.) can be used to denote the underworld itself. The answer to the question Juturna asks in lines 883–4 is, of course, 'no land'; there is no hope that she and Turnus will be able to be close to each other again.

885–6 Called 'mistress of ponds and rivers' at XII.139–40, Juturna was, indeed, a water-goddess worshipped at a number of cult sites in Rome (one in the Forum itself) and throughout Latium. There was a spring named Iuturna near the river Numicus (not far from where the fighting is taking place in *Aeneid* XII): it is probably to this river, her own, that she now retires in great sorrow and despair.

885 tantum: accusative neuter singular object of **effata**; 'this much and no more', or perhaps 'so much'. **glauco ... amictu:** ablative of means, with **contexit**. The colour of the cloak is appropriate for a water divinity. The covering of the head is a gesture of grief (cf. 870–1n.).

886 multa: neuter accusative plural, internal accusative (843n.) after **gemens**; 'groaning a great deal'. **fluvio ... alto:** ablative of place where, after **se ... condidit**.

A
Level

887–952

Virgil now returns to the single combat between Aeneas and Turnus, where the focus of the narrative will remain until the end of the poem. Little seems to have happened in the combat since 790, except the Dira flying at Turnus in 865–8; but the warriors now move onto the offensive.

This final phase of the single combat has a clear structure: a pair of speeches (889–93, 894–5), followed by Turnus' failed attempt to hurl a rock at Aeneas (896–918); then, Aeneas' (contrastingly) successful spear-cast (919–29), followed by another pair of speeches (931–8, 947–9); the final action of the scene and the poem, Aeneas' consideration and delivery of a death-blow to Turnus, takes place before and after the second of the latter pair of speeches.

The pace of the narrative slows considerably in this passage (compared with 710–90), to dwell on the decisive actions in the combat. The language and style show a greater density of imagery and intensity of hyperbole as the epic reaches its climax.

887–95 Aeneas was last seen at 788–90, with his spear restored, facing Turnus (who had recovered his sword). Here he moves onto the attack, presumably taking advantage of Turnus being unnerved by the owl flying in his face (this experience is alluded to only obliquely: 895n.); certainly, Turnus is not coming forward himself (889). The exchange of words between combatants on the battlefield is a feature of ancient martial epic from the *Iliad* onwards.

887 **instat**: cf. 762, 783; Aeneas presses Turnus as before.

887–8 **telumque coruscat/ ingens arboreum**: the **telum** is Aeneas' spear (775–6n., 787). The adjectives indicate its great size: Virgil dwells on the weapon since it will be the next throw of this that will prove decisive in the combat (919–27). For now, Aeneas 'brandishes' it; it is in this attitude that we find him later at 919.

888 saevo ... pectore: ablative of description.

888–93 Aeneas' speech shows justifiable anger (cf. **fervida** 894, **ferox** 895) at Turnus' behaviour earlier in the Book (**mora** 889, **cursu** 890), but also an unappealing cruelty (cf. **saevo** 888), as he mocks Turnus by challenging him to find some way of escaping now (891–3).

889 nunc deinde: 'from now on' – in contrast to the previous phase of the single combat when (since Aeneas had already thrown his spear) Turnus was able to outrun him and thus delay a decisive clash.

890 certandum est: gerundive of obligation with impersonal passive; lit. 'an act of competing must take place': tr. 'we must compete'. **cursu** is ablative of means, and **saevis ... armis** of instrument, with this verb.

891 tete: a variant form of *te* (cf. **sese** 53).

891–2 contrahe quidquid/ sive animis sive arte vales: **quidquid** is a relative pronoun, and here neuter accusative singular (internal accusative: 843n.) after **vales** (cf. 798): 'in whatever respect you are strong'; **animis** and **arte** are both ablatives of respect. *id* should be understood as antecedent of **quidquid** (678–9n., 12n.), since it is required as the object of **contrahe**. Tr. 'whatever strength you have (either in courage or in skill), gather it together'.

892–3 opta: imperative, governing the infinitives **sequi** and **condere** in 893. The two possibilities of escape for Turnus in 892–3 are alternatives, so *-que* in 893 means 'or' (rather than 'and').

892 pennis: ablative of instrument, with **sequi**.

893 cava ... terra: ablative of place where.

894–5 Turnus does not respond in kind to Aeneas' words, but shows dignity and clear recognition of the terrible gravity of the situation.

A
Level

894   ille: Turnus. **caput quassans**: this gesture is compatible with a range of feelings; here, as often, it may suggest anger or melancholy, but the short direct speech of Turnus which follows is controlled and defiant, and perhaps his shake of the head also indicates that he (Turnus) is by this stage above the sort of verbal wrangling Aeneas has indulged in during the previous five lines.

895   ferox: a vocative, addressed to Aeneas. **di me terrent et Iuppiter hostis**: Turnus has recognized the significance of the Dira as a sign of Jupiter's opposition to him; **di** (a variant of the nominative plural *dei*) indicates that he thinks he has incurred the enmity of other gods as well.

896–914   Turnus sees a large rock lying nearby and attempts to throw it at Aeneas. (Unlike Aeneas, Turnus has not recovered the spear he threw at the start of their combat: 711n., 766–90n.) Throwing rocks is not beneath even the greatest of warriors in ancient epic, and they can be extremely effective in disabling or, indeed, killing opponents. But Turnus' throw is weak, and the rock falls short of its target.

897–8   saxum ... campo quod forte iacebat,/ limes agro positus: 'a rock ... which was by chance lying on the plain (**campo** ablative of place where), having been put in place as a boundary for a field'. Since **positus** must be referring to the **saxum**, we would expect it to be *positum* (nominative singular neuter, agreeing with **saxum** and **quod**); but the participle has here been attracted into the gender of the neighbouring noun **limes**, which is in apposition to **quod**. Cf. 817n.

898   litem ut discerneret arvis: as a boundary-stone, the rock was intended to decide a dispute over the plough-fields (*arvum* is, strictly speaking, ploughed land, as opposed to a meadow: acknowledging this in translation here avoids excessively repetitive English, after

campo and **agro** earlier in the sentence). The usage of **arvis** here is loose: it might be regarded as ablative of place where, or a difficult dative of personal interest – in which case, the expression would be elliptical, with **arvis** standing for 'owners of *arva*'.

899–900   The rock picked up by Turnus is so heavy that twelve men born nowadays would have difficulty lifting it.

899   **illum** must refer to the **saxum**, but the pronoun is masculine in gender (neuter would be *illud*) – apparently under the influence of **limes** in 898. **lecti bis sex**: 'twelve (lit. twice six) chosen men' (chosen, that is, for their strength). **cervice**: ablative of means, or place where, with **subirent** (potential subjunctive).

900   **qualia nunc hominum producit corpora tellus**: the antecedent (**hominum ... corpora**) of the relative clause (**qualia nunc ... producit ... tellus**) is drawn into the relative clause (48–9n.); **hominum ... corpora** is in apposition to **lecti bis sex** in 899. *corpus* is here used with a defining genitive to denote periphrastically what is the meaning of the noun in the genitive (**hominum ... corpora** means simply 'human beings'). Tr. '(twelve chosen men), human beings such as the earth now brings forth'.

901   **ille**: adversative asyndeton (663–4n.). **ille** is here an adjective: its noun **heros** only appears at the end of the next line. **manu ... trepida**: ablative of instrument, with **raptum**. **raptum**: understand *saxum* from 896–7 (*apo koinou*: 32–3n.). **torquebat**: the imperfect tense can be used of attempted action (the 'conative' imperfect); Turnus 'tried to send the rock spinning'.

902   **altior**: adjective used adverbially, with **insurgens**. **cursu concitus**: **concitus** is middle-passive (623–4n.: 'having set himself in motion'); tr. 'setting off at a run'. Turnus runs in an attempt to generate extra force behind his throw.

A Level

903   neque currentem se nec cognoscit euntem: the participles after **cognoscit** express the actual condition of the object (**se**); 'he did not recognize himself as he was running nor as he was going'. **euntem** here is not a mere restatement of **currentem**, but traces the slowing of Turnus' progress: he runs at first, but is unable to maintain this (cf. 905).

904   manu: ablative of instrument, with **tollentem** (the object of which is *saxum*, understood *apo koinou* (32–3n.) from the next participle phrase in the line).

905   genua labant: the reason is explained in the following clause. **gelidus concrevit frigore sanguis**: **gelidus** is proleptic (94n.), after **concrevit**. **frigore** is ablative of cause, with **concrevit**. Lit. 'his blood froze because of the cold, so that it became icy'. The 'cold' (**frigore**) which Turnus feels here is the chill of fear.

906   tum: 'moreover', as well as 'then'; not only was the force of Turnus' throw limited, the distance covered by the stone itself (**ipse**) was also (consequently) limited. **vacuum per inane**: **inane** is a noun here, 'space'.

907   Turnus' final martial action in the poem is a comprehensive failure.

908–12   Turnus' struggle to perform as expected is compared to 'our' experience of frustrated action in dreams. The use of first-person forms (**videmur** 909, **succidimus** 910) encourages the reader towards sympathy for Turnus' plight.

908   pressit: a true perfect ('has pressed upon').

909   nocte: 864n.

909–10   avidos extendere cursus/ velle videmur: avidos is 'transferred epithet' (859n.); it should logically apply to the subject of **videmur**, where it would have adverbial force with **velle**. Tr. 'we seem to want eagerly to keep on running'; the plural **cursus** is hard to convey in English ('acts of running'): it shows that the experience being described is a repeated one (cf. **conatibus** 910).

910   conatibus: 'attempts', that is, to keep running. **aegri** describes the implied *nos* who are the subject of **succidimus**.

911   non . . . valet: 'is weak'.

911–12   non corpore notae/ sufficiunt vires: 'the strength which we know we have (**notae**) in our body (**corpore** ablative of place where, or of specification) is not present'.

913–14   It emerges from these lines that the Dira is no longer acting simply as a harbinger of destruction (846–8n., 850n.), nor is she even content to weaken Turnus with fear (905n.); she is now actively hindering him from successfully attacking Aeneas. The nature of the Dira's intervention here is mysterious (how does she **successum . . . negat**?); this very lack of clarity only serves to render her an even more unsettling figure.

913   Turno: dative of indirect object after **negat** (914). **quacumque viam virtute petivit**: **quacumque** is an adverb here ('wherever', or 'in whatever manner'). **virtute**: ablative of means, with **petivit**. **viam**: not a literal 'route', but a 'way' of proceeding or of achieving something. Judging from these words, Turnus seems to have been trying to resist Aeneas in further ways, besides his attempt to throw the rock – but the Dira (914) prevented him from doing so.

914   dea dira: 'the dread goddess'; the combination of noun and epithet (instead of the single word Dira) emphasizes the power of the creature who is working against Turnus.

914–18   Turnus looks around desperately for support (915, 918); but he has no help, no escape and no way to attack Aeneas.

A
Level

914 **pectore**: ablative of place where.

915 **Rutulos**: last glimpsed at 861, and previously at 758–62; the situation is still essentially that presented at 704–9. **urbem**: Latinus' city, in front of which the single combat has been taking place.

916 **metu**: ablative of cause, with **cunctatur. letumque instare tremescit**: *tremesco* means 'I tremble', and in its transitive form usually takes an accusative of the thing trembled at; that usage is extended here, with an accusative and infinitive: 'he trembled (as he saw) that death was looming'.

917–18 The verb **videt** (918) governs both the indirect questions in 917 and the two accusative objects in 918; **videt** is literal with the latter and metaphorical with the former (32–3n.).

918 **currus**: presumably plural for singular, with Turnus looking for his own chariot – although conceivably he is looking around for any chariots at all. **aurigamve sororem**: Juturna. We know that she has departed (869–86).

919 **cunctanti**: deponent present participle (5n.); understand *Turno* or *ei*. The dative is used after **telum ... coruscat**, possibly by analogy with verbs of threatening (which typically take a dative of indirect object). **telum ... fatale coruscat**: Aeneas has been in this pose since 887–8. **telum**: Aeneas' spear (775–6n., 887–8n.). **fatale** here bears primarily the sense 'deadly', but with some element of 'ordained by fate'.

920 **sortitus fortunam**: 'choosing an opportunity'; perfect participles of deponent verbs can be used to express an action contemporaneous with the finite verb (here **coruscat**). **oculis**: ablative of means, with **sortitus. corpore toto**: ablative of means, with **intorquet**.

921 **intorquet**: understand as object *telum* from 919 (*apo koinou*: 32–3n.).

921-3 Virgil compares the noise made by Aeneas' spear as it hurtles through the air to the noise of rocks hurled from a war-machine and to a thunderclap; in fact, he says that the spear made even more noise than these things.

921-2 murali . . ./ tormento: ablative of instrument, with **concita**. *tormentum* is a general term for war-machines which discharge missiles; **murali** indicates that this particular machine is used to attack city walls: a large siege engine, therefore, which hurls rocks. **numquam/. . . sic saxa fremunt**: 'never in this way do rocks roar' (when the rocks from the *tormentum* rush through the air, that is); **numquam sic** means, in effect, 'never so loudly'.

922-3 nec fulmine tanti/ dissultant crepitus: 'nor do such great crashing sounds burst at a thunderbolt'. **fulmine** could be ablative of place where, of origin or of cause.

923 volat atri turbinis instar: **instar** with genitive compares an action or a thing to something else, and suggests that it rivals or matches that other thing in terms of its effect, weight, size or type. The simplest English translation is 'like'; but a more accurate representation of the word is given by 'flew with the force of a dark whirlwind'.

924-5 orasque recludit/ loricae et clipei extremos septemplicis orbes: the moment of impact; the spear pierces (**recludit**) 'the edges of the corselet and the furthest-back circular layers of the seven-layered shield'. Turnus carries a massive shield, which has seven layers (of hide or metal, or both) and is round in shape. Its **extremos . . . orbes** are usually taken to be 'the furthest-out circles' from the centre – that is, its outermost rim, where the shield would be least thick; but **extremos** is perhaps better understood as 'furthest-back' (furthest from Aeneas), with the phrase **extremos . . . orbes** denoting the circular layers of the shield which are closest to Turnus' body. Either

A
Level

way, it is striking that Virgil presents the two breachings of Turnus'
armour in reverse order (corselet, then shield – when the spear would
pierce shield before reaching the body armour): the technique of
narrating a later event prior to an earlier one is known as *hysteron
proteron*, and serves to place emphasis on the action which is promoted
forwards in the sentence.

926   stridens describes the *hasta* (understood from 924 as the
subject of **transit**).

927   duplicato poplite: the ablative absolute clarifies how Turnus
fell down (**incidit** 927) to the ground; after Aeneas' spear had pierced
his thigh, that leg naturally gave way and he was forced to sink down
'with bended knee'.

928   gemitu: 'comitative' ablative ('with groaning'), with **consurgunt**
(which incidentally implies that the spectators of the single combat
have been sitting down at least for a period prior to this).

929   mons: there are various low hills close to the area where Latinus'
city appears to be placed, not far in from the coast (cf. XI.522–31);
Virgil may refer to one of these. Alternatively he may have in mind
the *mons Albanus* (the dominant peak of the Alban Hills in Latium),
from which Juno watched the preparations for the single combat
at XII.134–7; that *mons* is more than ten miles from Latinus' city,
and the suggestion that so distant a mountain might 're-echo' the
Rutulians' groaning would involve some hyperbole. **circum**: adverb,
with **remugit** 928. **vocem**: the noise uttered by the Rutulians and
characterized in 928 as **gemitu**. **late**: 'across a wide area'. **nemora alta**:
it is clear from parts of *Aeneid* XI that there are large wooded areas
not far from Latinus' city (XI.515, 522–31, 896–905).

930   humilis supplex: both nominative singular adjectives, to be
taken with **ille**.

A
Level

930–1 oculos dextramque precantem/ protendens: protendens ('stretching forth') makes clearer sense with **dextram precantem** as object than it does with **oculos** (where an idea of 'lifting' seems to be required); such a use of a single word to mean different things when it is taken with different parts of a sentence is called 'zeugma'. Here Turnus attempts to bolster his words (931–8) with such physical gestures of supplication as he can manage in his injured state.

931–8 Turnus acknowledges Aeneas' victory, and appeals for pity – at least for his father Daunus.

931 merui: 'I have deserved (this)'; there is no object, but it is clear from **utere sorte tua** in the next line that Turnus means he has deserved to be at Aeneas' mercy. Some have seen this word as an admission of moral guilt from Turnus (for leading the resistance against the Trojans); but more probably he simply means that having lost the combat he has deserved to be at Aeneas' mercy.

932 utere: 43n.; *utor* takes an ablative object (hence **sorte tua**). **tua. miseri**: adversative asyndeton (663–64n.). **miseri . . . parentis**: objective genitive after **si qua . . ./ . . . cura** ('if any concern for a wretched parent').

933 oro: parenthetical (cf. 72–3n., 777n.).

933–4 fuit et tibi talis/ Anchises genitor: tibi is possessive dative (lit. 'there was also (**et**) belonging to you . . .'; tr. 'you also had such a father'). Anchises is an important character in Books II and III of the *Aeneid* (where Aeneas tells how he rescued his father from Troy, and how Anchises helped to guide the Trojans across the eastern Mediterranean before dying in western Sicily); in Book VI, Aeneas goes to see him in the underworld. Aeneas is deeply attached to his father, even in death; Turnus' appeal is therefore an effective one. **talis** means primarily that Anchises was of similar age to Turnus' father Daunus (anticipating **senectae** 934).

A
Level

934   **Dauni**: 22n. **miserere senectae**: 43n.

935–6   **et me, seu corpus spoliatum lumine mavis,/ redde meis**: **seu** can be used to introduce some qualification of a preceding word (*OLD* 9), here **me**, and to suggest an alternative to that word; 'and give me – or, if you prefer, my body robbed of life (62–3n.) – back to my people (cf. 653n.)'.

936–7   **victum tendere palmas/ Ausonii videre**: understand *me* with **victum**; the construction is accusative ([*me*] **victum**) and infinitive (**tendere**) after a verb of perceiving. **Ausonii**: 834n. **videre**: 12n.

938   **ne tende**: 72–3n. **odiis**: ablative of respect; **ulterius** is a comparative adverb (contrast 806): 'do not press on any further in hatred'.

938–52   Aeneas is affected by Turnus' speech, and holds himself back. But then he sees a sword-belt which Turnus is wearing – a trophy Turnus seized from Pallas after killing him in Book X. Pallas was the son of Evander, the Trojans' first ally in Italy. (Cf. p. 9.) Aeneas was furious when Pallas was killed (X.510–605), and that rage now returns (946–7, 951) as he is reminded of his friend and dependant's death. Unwilling or unable to control his feelings, Aeneas plunges his sword into Turnus' chest.

938   **stetit**: the verb indicates that Aeneas has paused; it also marks a contrast with Turnus' abject posture.

939   **volvens oculos**: this gesture could indicate a range of feelings; probably here it suggests a combination of fierce concentration and perplexity. **dextramque repressit**: Aeneas 'checked' his right hand, either from seizing his sword or (more likely) from bringing up to kill Turnus that sword which it was already holding.

**A
Level**

940-1 **iam iamque magis cunctantem flectere sermo/ coeperat**: with **cunctantem**, understand *Aenean* or *eum*. **iam iamque**: 754n. **magis** should probably be taken with **cunctantem** rather than with **flectere**. Tr. 'the speech had been about to begin to prevail upon him, as he was delaying more and more'.

941 **infelix**: 'unlucky', in that the sword-belt (942) brings misfortune to Turnus; also, perhaps, 'bringing unhappiness', in that it reminds Aeneas of Pallas' death. **umero . . . alto**: ablative of place where; 'high on his shoulder'.

942 **balteus**: a sword-belt, worn over the shoulder. **notis . . . bullis**: ablative of means, with **fulserunt**. The *bullae* are the round studs on Pallas' sword-belt (**cingula**, plural for singular); they are 'known' to Aeneas since they belonged to his friend.

943 **Pallantis pueri**: 938-52n. The *Aeneid* uses both *iuvenis* and *puer* of Pallas – the latter when (as here) Virgil wishes to emphasize Pallas' youth.

943-4 **victum quem vulnere Turnus/ straverat**: **vulnere** is ablative of means, with **victum** (which agrees with **quem**). At X.482-9, Pallas collapses in death immediately after being wounded by Turnus' spear-cast.

944 **atque umeris inimicum insigne gerebat**: strictly this clause is additional to the preceding relative clause, rather than being part of that clause; the construction is loose but comprehensible. **insigne** is here a noun, meaning 'trophy'; it refers to Pallas' sword-belt. **umeris** is ablative of place where.

945 **ille**: the narrator returns to Aeneas, after four lines focusing on the sword-belt. **oculis**: ablative of means, with **hausit** (946). Aeneas 'looked long at' (lit. 'took in with his eyes') the sword-belt.

**A
Level**

945–6 **saevi monimenta doloris/ exuviasque**: the *-que* here is epexegetic (*OLD* 6), meaning it adds a word (**exuvias**) which explains what came before; Aeneas looked at 'the reminders of a savage grief – (that is,) the spoils'. The spoils (the sword-belt of Pallas which Turnus is wearing) are the thing which reminds Aeneas of the savage grief he felt when Pallas was killed (938–52n.).

946–7 **furiis accensus et ira/ terribilis**: **accensus** and **terribilis** both describe **ille** (946); there is no verb (but see 947–9n.). **furiis** (here perhaps more 'avenging rage' than 'frenzy', although the two may overlap) is ablative of respect, with **accensus**. **ira**: ablative of cause, with **terribilis**.

947–9 The absence of a verb introducing this short speech – indeed, of any verb after the nominatives **accensus** and **terribilis** – speeds up the narrative at this crucial moment.

947 **hinc**: 'from here', probably in the sense of 'from this situation'. **spoliis indute meorum**: *induo* takes an ablative (**spoliis**) of what one dresses oneself in (*OLD* 4). The perfect passive participle **indute** is vocative, where we would expect a nominative agreeing with *tu* as the subject of **eripiare** (948): such attraction into the vocative is occasionally found in direct, lively questions such as this. **meorum** ('of my people': cf. 653n.) is a deliberate overstatement: the spoils came from Pallas alone, but Aeneas treats them as belonging to a wider group of his supporters.

948 **eripiare**: second-person singular present passive subjunctive (33n.); probably a true passive ('be snatched away'), although possibly a middle-passive (623–4n.) meaning 'escape'. The subjunctive is used within a 'repudiating deliberative' question: 'are you to be snatched away?'. **mihi**: dative of personal interest; here tr. 'from me'.

948–9 Aeneas tells Turnus not simply that Pallas is avenged by his (Aeneas') blow, but that Pallas himself should be understood as in some sense the agent who strikes the blow and exacts his own revenge.

948 hoc vulnere: the death-wound which Aeneas is about to inflict (950–1), rather than the wound already delivered (926–7).

949 immolat: this (usually technical) term presents Turnus' death as a 'sacrifice' – that is, as a religious act (or a hideous parody of one). **poenam scelerato ex sanguine sumit**: 'exacts punishment from your criminal blood'. Aeneas clearly considers Turnus' killing of Pallas to have been a crime (*scelus*), but his judgement is affected by his own feelings for the victim; in fact, the killing took place on the battlefield in wartime.

950 ferrum: his sword (16n.). **adverso sub pectore**: 'inside the chest which faced him'. Turnus has not turned away in fear.

951 fervidus: here used adverbially with **condit** (950): tr. 'angrily' or 'with blazing anger'. **illi**: Turnus; possessive dative (867n.). **frigore**: 'comitative' ablative. Turnus' limbs were made slack, 'with cold' (the chill, that is, of death: contrast **frigore** in 905).

952 vita: 'life' in the sense of 'that which animates a person' (*OLD* 4). **indignata**: the action of the participle is contemporaneous with the main verb **fugit** (920n.). Turnus' **vita** is resentful primarily because it is having to leave his body when he is still young. **sub umbras**: 'down to the underworld'.

On the ending of the poem, see pp. 17–18.

A Level

Vocabulary

An asterisk * denotes a word in OCR's Defined Vocabulary List for AS Latin.

*ab (+ *ablative*)	from
abruptum, -i *n.*	steep slope
in abruptum	into the steep; straight down
absisto, absistere, abstiti	I move apart; I burst forth (102); I cease (676)
ac	see atque
*accedo, accedere, accessi, accessum	I come up
accendo, accendere, accendi, accensum	I set aflame
*accipio, accipere, accepi, acceptum	I receive; I hear
*acer, acris, acre	fierce; vigorous
acerbus -a -um	bitter
*acies, aciei *f.*	battle-line
Actor, Actoris *m.*	Actor
actus, -us *m.*	impulse, momentum
acuo, acuere, acui, acutum	I make sharp, intensify
*ad (+ *accusative*)	to, towards, onto; at, beside, near (849); in preparation for (106); in reply to (631)
*addo, addere, addidi, additum	I attach (to), fit (onto)
*adduco, adducere, adduxi, adductum	I draw in, draw taut
*adeo	see usque adeo
*adeo, adire, adi(v)i, aditum	I go to
adfor, adfari, adfatus sum	I address, speak to
*adhuc (*adverb*)	still
*adicio, adicere, adieci, adiectum	I contribute
*adimo, adimere, ademi, ademptum	I remove, take away

adiuro, adiurare, adiuravi, adiuratum	I swear by
*adloquor, adloqui, adlocutus sum	I speak to
adnitor, adniti, adnixus sum	I lean on, lean against
adnuo, adnuere, adnui, adnutum (+ *dative*)	I nod assent to
adsisto, adsistere, adstiti	I take up my position
*adsum, adesse, adfui	I am at hand
*adversus -a -um	turned against; adverse, bad (1); directly facing (651, 950)
aedes, aedium *f. pl.*	(pl.) house, abode
aeger, aegra, aegrum	afflicted, sick (850); weary, exhausted (910)
aegresco, aegrescere	I become sick; I grow worse
Aeneadae, Aeneadum *m. pl.*	the followers of Aeneas
Aeneas, Aeneae *m.*	Aeneas
aeque (*adverb*)	to the same degree
aequo, aequare, aequavi, aequatum	I make level, balance
aequor, aequoris *n.*	level surface; plain (614, 710)
*aequus -a -um	right, just
aerius -a -um	up in the air
aes, aeris *n.*	bronze
aestuo, aestuare, aestuavi, aestuatum	I seethe
aeternus -a -um	eternal
aether, aetheris *m.*	upper air, sky
*affero, afferre, attuli, allatum	I bring, bring to
age	see **ago**
*ager, agri *m.*	field
agito, agitare, agitavi, agitatum	I drive on; I pursue, hound (803); I stimulate, I trouble (668)
*agmen, agminis *n.*	line of march, column; (sing. or pl.) line of troops, army
agnosco, agnoscere, agnovi, agnitum	I recognize
*ago, agere, egi, actum age (*imperative*)	I drive, drive on; I lead; I do come on; come now (832)
aio, ais, ait (*defective verb*)	I say, speak
ala, -ae *f.*	wing

Albanus -a -um	Alban, belonging to Alba Longa
albeo, albere	I am white
albus -a -um	white; pale
ales, alitis *m./f.*	bird
aliter (*adverb*)	differently
***alius, alia, aliud**	other, another
***alter, altera, alterum**	the other (of two); any other (639); another (830n.)
***altus -a -um**	high, tall; deep
amarus -a -um	bitter
Amata, -ae *f.*	Amata
ambo, ambae, ambo	both
amens (*genitive* **amentis**)	out of one's mind, frantic
amictus, -us *m.*	cloak
***amor, amoris** *m.*	love
amplius (*adverb*)	any further, any longer
an	was it really . . .? (conveys indignation or surprise, introducing direct questions)
Anchises, Anchisae *m.*	Anchises
anhelus -a -um	breathless; out of breath; causing breathlessness (790n.)
anima, -ae *f.*	soul, disembodied spirit (648)
***animus, -i** *m.*	mind; goodwill, generosity (23); (sing. or pl.) courage (19, 892); (pl.) spirits (4)
***annus, -i** *m.*	year
***ante** (+ *accusative*)	before
ante (*adverb*)	beforehand
***anteeo, anteire, antei(v)i, anteitum**	I go ahead; I surpass
antiquus -a -um	ancient
***aperio, aperire, aperui, apertum**	I open; I disclose, reveal
***appareo, apparere, apparui, apparitum**	I appear; I am noticed, I show myself (941); I am in attendance (850)
Appenninus, -i *m.*	Appenninus
apto, aptare, aptavi, aptatum	I adjust
***arbor, arboris** *f.*	tree

arboreus -a -um	tree-like
arcus, -us *m.*	bow
Ardea, -ae *f.*	Ardea
ardeo, ardere, arsi	I burn, I am on fire
ardeo in (+ *accusative*)	I burn for (71)
arduus -a -um	high, towering
aries, arietis *m.*	ram, battering-ram
*arma, -orum *n. pl.*	arms, weapons; military activities, fighting (844)
arma moveo	I go to fight (6)
armentum, -i *n.*	herd
armo, armare, armavi, armatum	I arm
armus, -i *m.*	shoulder
arrigo, arrigere, arrexi, arrectum	I make to stand on end (868); I prick up (618n.); I excite (731)
*ars, artis *f.*	skill; trick (632), stratagem (874)
arvum, -i *n.*	field; plough-field (898); (sing. or pl.) ground (681)
arx, arcis *f.*	citadel
ascio, ascire	I admit, receive
Asia, -ae *f.*	Asia
*aspecto, aspectare, aspectavi, aspectatum	I look towards
aspicio, aspicere, aspexi, aspectum	I see
ast	but
*asto, astare, astiti	I stand by, stand there
astrum, -i *n.*	star
*at	but
ater, atra, atrum	dark
Athos, Athonis *m.*	Athos
Atinas, Atinae *m.*	Atinas
atque or ac	and; and indeed (710); than (856)
*attollo, attollere	I raise up
*audax (*genitive* audacis)	bold
*audeo, audere, ausus sum	I dare; I dare to undertake
*audio, audire, audivi, auditum	I hear
aura, -ae *f.*	breeze, wind; (pl.) air, air of the sky
auriga, -ae *m.*	charioteer
auris, auris *f.*	ear

Aurora, -ae *f.*	Dawn (the goddess)
aurum, -i *n.*	gold
Auruncus -a -um	Auruncan
Ausonius -a -um	Ausonian
Ausonii, -orum *m. pl.*	the Ausonians
***aut**	or; nor (825)
aut . . . aut . . .	either . . . or . . .
***autem**	but; and; and indeed
avello, avellere, avelli, avulsum	I tear away
aversus -a -um	hostile; alienated
avidus -a -um	eager
avus, avi *m.*	ancestor
balteus, -i *m.*	sword-belt
bellator, bellatoris *m.*	warrior
***bellum, -i** *n.*	war
***bis**	twice
***bonus -a -um**	good; kind, kindly (777)
bulla, -ae *f.*	round stud
bustum, -i *n.*	tomb
caecus -a -um	unseen; with no clear cause (617)
***caelum, -i** *n.*	sky; heaven
calefacio, calefacere, calefeci,	I make hot
calefactum	
calidus -a -um	hot
***campus, -i** *m.*	plain, field
candeo, candere, candui	I am white-hot
candor, candoris *m.*	whiteness
***canis, canis** *m./f.*	dog
***cano, canere, cecini, cantum**	I sing; I prophesy (28)
***capio, capere, cepi, captum**	I take, capture
captiva, -ae *f.*	prisoner, captive
capulus, -i *m.*	sword-hilt
***caput, capitis** *n.*	head; source (816)
***carus -a -um**	dear
cassus -a -um	fruitless
casus, -us *m.*	outcome (23, 61); misfortune (32)
cavus -a -um	hollow; cupped (86)
***cedo, cedere, cessi, cessum**	I withdraw, yield; I pass to (as a possession) (17)

celebro, celebrare, celebravi, celebratum	I honour with ceremonies
honores celebro	I perform ceremonies of honour
*celer, celeris, celere	swift
*cerno, cernere, crevi, cretum	I decide the matter
*certamen, certaminis *n.*	conflict, struggle, contest
certatim	eagerly
certe (*adverb*)	for sure
certo, certare, certavi, certatum	I compete
certo de	I compete for, fight for
cervix, -icis *f.*	neck
cervus, -i *m.*	stag
*ceterus -a -um	the rest of
ceu	like
cieo, ciere, civi, citum	I set in motion; I raise, produce
*cingo, cingere, cinxi, cinctum	I surround
cingulum, -i *n.*	sword-belt
circa (*adverb*)	round about
*circum (+ *accusative*)	around
circum (*adverb*)	round about
*circumdo, circumdare, circumdedi, circumdatum	I put around
circumspicio, circumspicere, circumspexi, circumspectum	I look round and see
*circumsto, circumstare, circumsteti	I stand around
*clamor, clamoris *m.*	shout, shouting; din
claudo, claudere, clausi, clausum	I close; I enclose; I conceal
clipeus, -i *m.*	shield
*coeo, coire, coi(v)i, coitum	I come together; I meet
inter se coire	to join battle
*coepi, coepisse, coeptum	I begin
cognatus -a -um	kindred, belonging to kin
cognomen, cognominis *n.*	name
*cognosco, cognoscere, cognovi, cognitum	I recognize
me cognosco	I recognize myself
*colligo, colligere, collegi, collectum	I gather together; (passive) I shrink myself

collum, -i *n.*	neck
*colo, colere, colui, cultum	I carry out
color, coloris *m.*	colour
columna, -ae *f.*	column
coma, -ae *f.*	lock of hair; (sing. or pl.) hair
comans (*gen.* comantis)	hairy (6–7n.); fine-maned (86)
*comes, comitis *m./f.*	companion
comes eo	I go as a companion, I accompany (879)
comminus	at close quarters
commisceo, commiscere, commiscui, commixtum	I mix together, mix up with, mingle
*committo, committere, commisi, commissum	see **manum committo**
communis -is -e	shared, belonging to all
compingo, compingere, compegi, compactum	I fix together
compleo, complere, complevi, completum	I fill
*compono, componere, composui, compositum	I arrange, settle
conatus, -us *m.*	attempt
concieo, conciere, concivi, concitum	I set in motion; I hurl (921); (passive) I set myself in motion, I set off (902)
concipio, concipere, concepi, conceptum	I strike, draw up
concresco, concrescere, concrevi	I harden; I freeze
*concurro, concurrere, concurri, concursum	I run together, charge (724); I engage in battle, fight (771)
condicio, condicionis *f.*	law
*condo, condere, condidi, conditum	I hide; I bury
me condo	I hide myself, I vanish
*confero, conferre, contuli, collatum	see **manum confero**
*confundo, confundere, confudi, confusum	I throw into confusion, throw into turmoil; I bewilder, overwhelm

congemino, congeminare, congeminavi, congeminatum	I redouble
congredior, congredi, congressus sum	I join battle, meet in battle
***conicio, conicere, conieci, coniectum**	I hurl
***coniunx, coniugis** *f.*	wife, bride
consanguineus -a -um	related by blood
conscendo, conscendere, conscendi, conscensum	I mount
conscius -a -um	conscious of oneself, aware of one's own worth; conscious of guilt (666–8n.)
***consulo, consulere, consului, consultum**	I advise
***consurgo, consurgere, consurrexi, consurrectum**	I rise up
***contego, contegere, contexi, contectum**	I cover
***contendo, contendere, contendi, contentum**	I draw (a bow); I shoot (an arrow)
conterritus -a -um	very alarmed
***contra** (+ *accusative*)	facing (790)
contra (*adverb*)	against an opponent (887); in opposition (to this), in response (760); in reply (807); on the other hand (779)
***contraho, contrahere, contraxi, contractum**	I gather together
conubium, -i *n.*	marriage; (pl.) marriage ceremony
convello, convellere, convelli, convulsum	I tear out
***converto, convertere, converti, conversum**	I turn; I turn to face; I turn into
cor, cordis *n.*	heart
cornu, cornus *n.*	horn; socket (88–9n.)
corona, -ae *f.*	circle, ring
***corpus, corporis** *n.*	body

*corripio, corripere, corripui, correptum	I seize
corusco, coruscare, coruscavi	I make something flash by moving it; I brandish
coruscus -a -um	quivering, flickering
crastinus -a -um	of tomorrow, tomorrow's
creber, crebra, crebrum	frequent
crepitus, -us *m.*	crashing sound
cresco, crescere, crevi, cretum	I grow; I swell
*crimen, criminis *n.*	accusation
crinis, -is *m.*	a lock of hair; (pl.) hair
crista, -ae *f.*	crest, plume
*crudelis -is -e	cruel
cruentus -a -um	bloody
culmen, culminis *n.*	rooftop
*culpa, -ae *f.*	sense of guilt; wrongdoing (648n.)
*cum	when
cum iam	at that time when
cum primum	as soon as
cunctor, cunctari, cunctatus sum	I delay
*cur	why
*cura, -ae *f.*	concern, anxiety
*curro, currere, cucurri, cursum	I run
currus, -us *m.*	chariot
cursus, -us *m.*	running; speed
(rapido) cursu	at a (swift) run (683, 763, 902)
Cydon, Cydonis *m.*	a Cydonian
damno, damnare, damnavi, damnatum	I doom
Dardanides, Dardanidae *m.*	descendant of Dardanus; Trojan
Dardanius -a -um	descendant of Dardanus; Trojan (14–15n.)
Daunius -a -um	born of Daunus
Daunus, -i *m.*	Daunus
*de (+ *ablative*)	from, down from; for (765, see certo de)
*dea, deae *f.*	goddess
*debeo, debere, debui, debitum	I owe; (passive) I am destined for (795)

debilis -is -e	weak, without strength
decerno, decernere, decrevi, decretum	I decide the matter
decet, decere, decuit (*impersonal verb*)	it is right
decus, decoris *n.*	glory, honour
dedecus, dedecoris *n.*	dishonour, shame
***defendo, defendere, defendi, defensum**	I defend
defero, deferre, detuli, delatum	I carry down
deficio, deficere, defeci, defectum	I lose heart
deformo, deformare, deformavi, deformatum	I disfigure
dehinc	then, next
dehisco, dehiscere	I gape
***deicio, deicere, deieci, deiectum**	I cast down
***deinde**	see **nunc deinde**
***demitto, demittere, demisi, demissum**	I send down; I let go down (884)
demum	see **tum demum**
***denique**	in the end
densus -a -um	densely packed
***depono, deponere, deposui, depositum**	I lay aside, lay down
deprecor, deprecari, deprecatus sum	I beg to escape
***descendo, descendere, descendi, descensum**	I go down, come down
desero, deserere, deserui, desertum	I leave behind, abandon
desertor, -oris *m.*	abandoner
desertus -a -um	empty; deserted
***desino, desinere, desi(v)i, desitum**	I cease
desisto, desistere, destiti, destitum	I cease
desum, deesse, defui	I am lacking
***deus, dei** (*nominative pl.* **dei** or **di**) *m.*	god
***dextra, -ae** *f.*	right hand
***dico, dicere, dixi, dictum**	I say, speak
dictum, -i *n.*	word

*dignus -a -um	worthy, suitable
*dimitto, dimittere, dimisi, dimissum	I send away, discharge; I dismiss
Dira, -ae *f.*	Dira
dirimo, dirimere, diremi, diremptum	I decide, settle
*dirus -a -um	dreadful, dread
*discedo, discedere, discessi, discessum	I depart; I part
discerno, discernere, discrevi, discretum	I settle, decide
discludo, discludere, disclusi, disclusum	I prise open
discrimen, discriminis *n.*	distinction
discutio, discutere, discussi, discussum	I shake apart; I dispel
disicio, disicere, disieci, disiectum	I scatter
dissilio, dissilire, dissilui	I shatter
dissulto, dissultare	I leap apart, burst
*diu	for a long time
diversus -a -um	different; distant
*divido, dividere, divisi, divisum	I keep separate
divus, -i *m.*	god
*do, dare, dedi, datum	I give; I give over to, consign to (655); I grant (someone) the power (to do something) (97); I show (69); I utter (81); I make (681)
me do in (+ *accusative*)	I devote myself to (633)
*dolor, doloris *m.*	pain; distress, grief
*dolus, -i *m.*	trick
*domus, -us *m.* (*accusative pl.* domus *or* domos)	house; household (59, 805)
*donum, -i *n.*	gift
Drances, Drancis *m.*	Drances
dudum	previously
dulcis -is -e	sweet
*dum	while; as long as
*duo, duae, duo	two

duplico, duplicare, duplicavi, duplicatum	I bend double, bend
*durus -a -um	hard, harsh; enduring, suffering (873n.)
*e or ex (+ *ablative*)	from, out of; as a result of; after
ebur, eboris *n.*	ivory
ecce	look! (650n.)
edo, esse, edi, esum	I eat; I eat away at, consume
educo, educere, eduxi, eductum	I raise, extend upward
efflagito, efflagitare, efflagitavi, efflagitatum	I demand
effor, effari, effatus sum	I speak
*ego, mei	I, me
ei mihi	alas!
eludo, eludere, elusi, elusum	I mock
emico, emicare, emicavi, emicatum	I rush forwards
eminus	from a distance
*enim	for
ensis, ensis *m.*	sword
*eo, ire, i(v)i, itum	I go
equidem	for my part; in truth
*equus, -i *m.*	horse
*ergo	and so, therefore
*eripio, eripere, eripui, ereptum	I snatch away from, snatch up
me eripio	I snatch myself away from, I escape (917)
Eryx, Erycis *m.*	Eryx
esto	so be it, may it be so (821)
*et	and; too; as (846)
et ... et ...	both ... and ...
Eurus, -i *m.*	the East Wind
evado, evadere, evasi, evasum	I pass right through
everbero, everberare, everberavi, everberatum	I beat violently, keep beating
*ex (+ *ablative*)	see e
examen, examinis *n.*	tongue belonging to a pair of scales
*excedo, excedere, excessi, excessum	I withdraw, go away
excidium, -ii *n.*	destruction

excido, excidere, excidi, excisum	I cut down; I destroy, raze (762)
***exclamo, exclamare, exclamavi, exclamatum**	I shout out
excutio, excutere, excussi, excussum	I shake out
exim	then, next
***exitium, -ii** *n.*	destruction
***exorior, exoriri, exortus sum**	I rise up
exosus -a -um (+ *accusative*)	hating
expendo, expendere, expendi, expensum	I weigh up
expleo, explere, explevi, expletum	I complete
exscindo, exscindere, exscindi, exscissum	I destroy
exstinguo, exstinguere, exstinxi, exstinctum	I kill
exsulto, exsultare, exsultavi	I bound, leap; I show unrestrained pleasure, rejoice
***exsupero, exsuperare, exsuperavi, exsuperatum**	I excel (20); I mount up, rise up (46)
extendo, extendere, extendi, extentum/extensum	I prolong, keep on
exterritus -a -um	terrified
extremus -a -um	furthest, the furthest part of; furthest back (924–5n.)
exuviae, -arum *f. pl.*	spoils
facies, faciei *f.*	form, shape, appearance
***facio, facere, feci, factum**	I make
***fallo, fallere, fefelli, falsum**	I escape notice, go unnoticed (634, 877)
***fama, -ae** *f.*	rumour; story
fama est	the story is (that . . .), it is said (that . . .)
fas *n.* (*indeclinable*)	right (in the eyes of the gods)
fatalis -is -e	ordained by fate; deadly
fateor, fateri, fassus sum	I acknowledge
fatum, -i *n.*	(sing. or pl.) fate, destiny
fauces, faucium *f. pl.*	throat
Faunus, -i *m.*	Faunus

fax, facis *f.*	firebrand
fel, fellis *n.*	venom
***felix** (*genitive* **felicis**)	lucky; well-omened; successful
femineus -ea -eum	womanish
femur, feminis/femoris *n.*	thigh
ferio, ferire	I strike
***fero, ferre, tuli, latum**	I bring, carry; I endure; I bear (a child) (847); (passive) I rush (855)
me fero	I make my way (860, 865–6)
***ferox** (*genitive* **ferocis**)	fierce, fierce-spirited; ferocious, savage
ferreus -a -um	of iron
***ferrum, -i** *n.*	iron, steel; sword (16n.); spear-point (774, 777; cf. 50)
fervidus -a -um	seething, hot; blazing (with anger), angry
fido, fidere, fisus sum (+ *dative or ablative*)	I trust in
fidus -a -um (+ *genitive*)	loyal to
figo, figere, fixi, fixum	I fix in, lodge in; I fix on; I fasten (768)
figura, -ae *f.*	shape
finio, finire, finivi, finitum	I put an end to
***finis, finis** *m./f.*	end
***fio, fieri**	I become
flagro, flagrare, flagravi	I burn, blaze
***flamma, -ae** *f.*	flame
flecto, flectere, flexi, flexum	I bend, turn; I make to abate (46), prevail upon (940)
me flecto	I bend my steps, turn (658)
fleo, flere, flevi, fletum	I weep
fluctus, -us *m.*	wave
fluentum, -i *n.*	flowing water
***flumen, fluminis** *n.*	river
fluvius, -ii *m.*	river
foedo, foedare, foedavi, foedatum	I defile; I disfigure
***foedus, foederis** *n.*	agreement, treaty
folium, -(i)i *n.*	leaf

fons, fontis *m.*	spring, spring-water
for, fari, fatus sum	I say, speak
formido, formidinis *f.*	fear, dread; a scare (750n.)
fors, (fortis) *f.*	chance, fortune
***forte** (*adverb*)	by chance
***Fortuna, -ae** *f.*	Fortuna, Fortune
***fortuna, -ae** *f.*	fortune; outcome (694); opportunity (920)
fragmen, fragminis *n.*	fragment
fragor, fragoris *m.*	crash
***frango, frangere, fregi, fractum**	I break
***frater, fratris** *m.*	brother
fremo, fremere, fremui, fremitum	I roar (8, 702, 922); snort, neigh (82)
***frigus, frigoris** *n.*	cold, chill
frons, frontis *f.*	forehead
***frustra** (*adverb*)	in vain; without justification
frustror, frustrari, frustratus sum	I disappoint
***fuga, -ae** *f.*	flight
fugax (*genitive* **fugacis**)	fleeing, running away
***fugio, fugere, fugi**	I flee; I flee from
fulgeo, fulgere, fulsi	I shine out, gleam
fulmen, fulminis *n.*	thunderbolt
fulmino, fulminare, fulminavi, fulminatum	I thunder
fulvus -a -um	yellow; dull yellow (792)
***fundo, fundere, fudi, fusum**	I pour; I shed
funus, funeris *n.*	death
furia, -ae *f.*	(usually pl.) madness, frenzy; avenging rage
furo, furere	I am mad; I behave madly
***furor, furoris** *m.*	madness; frenzied behaviour (832)
furorem furo	I pursue a mad course (680)
futtilis -is -e	brittle
***gaudeo, gaudere, gavisus sum**	I rejoice
gelidus -a -um	icy
geminus -a -um	twin, two born at the same birth
gemitus, -us *m.*	groan, groaning
gemo, gemere, gemui, gemitum	I groan, moan
gena, -ae *f.*	cheek

gener, generi *m.*	son-in-law; prospective son-in-law (31n.)
genitor, genitoris *m.*	father; the father (title given to Jupiter)
***gens, gentis** *f.*	race
genu, genus *n.*	knee
***genus, generis** *n.*	family, lineage; race
germana, -ae *f.*	sister
***gero, gerere, gessi, gestum**	I feel (48); I wield (97); I wear (944)
gigno, gignere, genui, genitum	I bring into being; (passive) I am born
glacies, glaciei *f.*	ice
***gladius, -(i)i** *m.*	sword
glaucus -a -um	grey-green
glisco, gliscere	I grow
gramen, graminis *n.*	grass
***gravis -is -e**	serious
habena, -ae *f.*	rein
***habeo, habere, habui, habitum**	I have; I have under my control (17); I wear (88)
hac (*adverb*)	in this direction
haereo, haerere, haesi, haesum	I stick close (754); I stick, am stuck (868); I linger (796)
harena, -ae *f.*	sand
***hasta, -ae** *f.*	spear
hastile, hastilis *n.*	spear
***haud**	not (9n.)
haudquaquam	in no way
haurio, haurire, hausi, haustum	I drink in; I take in (with my mind or senses) (26, 946)
heros, heroos *m.*	hero
***hic** (*adverb*)	here; at this point (728)
***hic, haec, hoc**	this
***hinc**	from here; from this origin (838)
hinc . . . hinc . . .	on one side . . . on the other side . . .
hio, hiare, hiavi	I gape, have my mouth wide open
***homo, hominis** *m.*	human being, man
***honos, honoris** *m.*	honour; regard (57); an act which bestows honour (778)

horrendus -a -um	terrifying
horreo, horrere, horrui	I bristle
horrificus -a -um	dreadful
horror, horroris *m.*	dread
*hostis, hostis *m.*	enemy
*huc	to this place, in this direction, this way
huc ... huc ...	this way ... that way ...
huc illuc	this way and that way
humilis -is -e	humbled; humble; on the ground
hymenaeus, -i *m.*	(usually pl.) a wedding, marriage
*iaceo, iacere, iacui, iacitum	I lie
*iam	now; already
iam iamque	at any time now (754n.)
icio, icere, ici, ictum	I strike
ictus, -us *m.*	blow
*idem, eadem, idem	the same
Idmon, Idmonis *m.*	Idmon
ignavus -a -um	cowardly
ignipotens (*genitive* **ignipotentis**)	lord of fire
*ignis, ignis *m.*	fire
ignotus -a -um	unknown, not recognized
ilex, ilicis *f.*	holm oak
Iliacus -a -um	Trojan
*ille, illa, illud	that; he, she, it; this particular person or thing (819)
olli	(see 18n., 788n.)
illuc	to that place, in that direction, that way
huc illuc	see **huc**
imago, imaginis *f.*	representation, picture
imber, imbris *m.*	rain
immanis -is -e	massive
immedicabilis -is -e	inflicting a wound that cannot be cured
immolo, immolare, immolavi, immolatum	I sacrifice
immortalis -is -e	immortal
impavidus -a -um	fearless

*impedio, impedire, impedi(v)i, impeditum	I hinder
*impello, impellere, impuli, impulsum	I strike; I discharge (856)
impense	carefully, earnestly
imperito, imperitare, imperitavi, imperitatum (+ *dative*)	I rule
*imperium, imperii *n.*	power; empire
*impetus, -us *m.*	force, momentum
impius -a -um	unholy
implacabilis -is -e	implacable
implico, implicare, implicavi, implicatum	I entwine (743n.)
imploro, implorare, imploravi, imploratum	I call for help
*impono, imponere, imposui, impositum	I place in
importunus -a -um	untimely; ill-omened
improbus -a -um	relentless
impune (*adverb*)	without punishment
impune esse	to go unpunished
imus -a -um	the lowest part(s) of
*in (+ *ablative*)	in, on; over (781)
*in (+ *accusative*)	into, onto; against; for (71, 103, 735); to (633), towards (656, 901); in order to be/produce (something) (780, 854)
inane, inanis *n.*	empty space (906)
inanis -is -e	empty
incertus -a -um	uncertain
*incido, incidere, incidi, incasum	I fall, fall down
*incipio, incipere, incepi, inceptum	I begin; I begin to speak (692)
inclino, inclinare, inclinavi, inclinatum	I make to lean
includo, includere, inclusi, inclusum	I hem in
incognitus -a -um	unrecognized
incolumis -is -e	unharmed, alive

increpo, increpare, increpui, increpitum	I snap (755); I snap at (758)
incumbo, incumbere, incubui	I exert myself
*incurro, incurrere, incurri, incursum	I run into, charge into
*inde	then
indecoris -is -e	inglorious, without honour
indigena, -ae *f.*	native person
indiges (*genitive* indigetis)	*Indiges* (title of a type of Roman divinity: 794–5n.)
indignor, indignari, indignatus sum	I am indignant (786), resentful (952)
indignus -a -um (+ *genitive*)	unworthy of; unsuitable
induo, induere, indui, indutum (+ *ablative*)	I clothe, dress in
Indus -a -um	Indian
inermis -is -e	unarmed, without a weapon
infandus -a -um	unspeakable
infelix (*genitive* infelicis)	ill-fated, luckless, wretched
inferior -ior -ius	inferior
infigo, infigere, infixi, infixum	I drive in
infit	he begins
inflecto, inflectere, inflexi, inflexum	I bend; I change, move
*infringo, infringere, infregi, infractum	I break
*ingens (*genitive* ingentis)	huge; mighty (640)
ingruo, ingruere, ingrui (+ *dative*)	I advance threateningly upon
inhibeo, inhibere, inhibui, inhibitum	I hold in check
inimicus -a -um	hostile (716, 812); belonging to an enemy (944)
inlaetabilis -is -e	dismal
innuptus -a -um	unmarried
*inquit	he says
insania, -ae *f.*	madness
inscius -a -um (+ *genitive*)	not knowing; innocent of (648n.)
*insequor, insequi, insecutus sum	I pursue
*insidiae, -arum *f. pl.*	trap

insigne, -is *n.*	decoration, trophy
insisto, insistere, institi	I set foot on; I begin
instar (+ *genitive*)	with the force of (923n.)
insterno, insternere, instravi, instratum	I lay on
insto, instare, institi	I press (in a hostile manner), press on; I apply myself urgently (783); I loom (916)
***insurgo, insurgere, insurrexi**	I rise up
intempestus -a -um	timeless
***inter** (+ *accusative*)	among, between
interdum	from time to time
***interea**	meanwhile
intono, intonare, intonui	I thunder
intorqueo, intorquere, intorsi, intortum	I send spinning; I hurl
invado, invadere, invasi, invasum	I charge into, plunge into (712)
***inveho, invehere, invexi, invectum**	I carry on
invisus -a -um	loathed, hated
***invitus -a -um**	unwilling
involvo, involvere, involvi, involutum	I roll along
***ipse, ipsa, ipsum**	himself, herself, itself; by himself, alone (843)
***ira, -ae** *f.*	anger
irascor, irasci	I am angry, I become angry; I throw my rage (104n.)
***is, ea, id**	he, she, it; that
iste, ista, istud	that
***ita**	thus, in this way
Italia, -ae *f.*	Italy
Italus -a -um	of Italy, Italian
Itali, -orum *m. pl.*	men of Italy, Italians
***iubeo, iubere, iussi, iussum**	I order
***iungo, iungere, iunxi, iunctum**	I yoke; I make (something) together with another, I make (something) to bind myself to another (822)
Iuno, Iunonis *f.*	Juno

Iuppiter, Iovis *m.*	Jupiter
iussum, -i *n.*	order, command
Iuturna, -ae *f.*	Juturna
iuvenca, -ae *f.*	heifer
***iuvenis, -is** *m.*	young man
***iuvo, iuvare, iuvi, iutum**	I help
labo, labare, labavi	I give way, am shaky
***labor, laboris** *m.*	struggle
lacero, lacerare, laceravi, laceratum	I rend, tear
lacesso, lacessere, lacessi(v)i, **lacessitum**	I rouse (85–6n.); I challenge (105)
lacrima, -ae *f.*	tear
lacus, -us *m.*	lake
laetor, laetari, laetatus sum	I rejoice, am delighted
laetitia, -ae *f.*	happiness, delight
***laetus -a -um**	happy
languidus -a -um	drowsy, weary
lanx, lancis *f.*	plate; pan belonging to a pair of scales, scale-pan
lapis, lapidis *m.*	stone
largus -a -um	abundant
Latinus, -i *m.*	Latinus
Latinus -a -um	of Latium, Latin
Latini, -orum *m. pl.*	men of Latium
Latium, -i *n.*	Latium
latratus, -us *m.*	barking
latro, -onis *m.*	robber, plunderer
***latus -a -um**	wide, broad
Laurens (*genitive* **Laurentis**)	Laurentine
***laus, laudis** *f.*	praise, glory
Lavinia, -ae *f.*	Lavinia
lavo, lavare, lavi, lavatum	I wash; I soak
***lego, legere, legi, lectum**	I choose, select
***lentus -a -um**	tough, clinging
leo, leonis *m.*	lion
letalis -is -e	belonging to death; deadly
letum, -i *n.*	death
***levis -is -e**	light; trivial
***lex, legis** *f.*	law

*liber, libera, liberum	free; subject to free choice (74)
*licet, licere, licuit/licitum est	it is permitted (786n.)
lignum, -i *n.*	wood; tree
lilium, lil(i)i *n.*	lily
limen, liminis *n.*	threshold
limes, limitis *m.*	boundary
lingua, -ae *f.*	tongue
linquo, linquere, liqui	I leave
lis, litis *f.*	dispute
longaevus -a -um	aged
longe (*adverb*)	at a distance, far off
longe sum (+ *dative*)	I am of no use to (52)
lorica, -ae *f.*	corselet
lorum, -i *n.*	leather strap; (pl.) reins
luctor, luctari, luctatus sum	I struggle
luctus, -us *m.*	grief
ludicer/ludicrus -cra -crum	belonging to sport
lumen, luminis *n.*	light; light of life, life
luo, luere, lui	I atone for
*lux, lucis *f.*	light; life (660, 873)
madeo, madere	I am wet, am soaked
maestus -a -um	sorrowing, sad
*magis (*adverb*)	more, the more
*magister, magistri *m.*	master; herd-master (717)
magnanimus -a -um	great-hearted
*magnus -a -um	great
maiestas, maiestatis *f.*	grandeur, greatness
mala, -ae *f.*	jaw
*malo, malle, malui	I prefer
*maneo, manere, mansi, mansum	I stay; I await (61–2)
Manes, Manium *m. pl.*	spirits of the dead (646–7n.); the underworld (884n.)
*manus, -us *f.*	hand; fighting (23n., 627, 629)
manum confero (+ *dative*)	I join battle with
manum committo (+ *dative*)	I join battle with
Mars, Martis *m.*	Mars (god of war); war (1n.)
*mater, matris *f.*	mother
medeor, mederi	I heal, try to heal
*medius -a -um	the middle of

Megaera, -ae *f.*	Megaera
membrum, -i *n.*	limb
***mens, mentis** *f.*	mind
mereo, merere, merui, meritum	I deserve
mereor, mereri, meritus sum	I deserve; I deserve punishment (852)
Messapus, -i *m.*	Messapus
Metiscus, -i *m.*	Metiscus
metuo, metuere, metui	I fear
***metus, -us** *m.*	fear
***meus -a -um**	my
mico, micare, micavi	I flicker
***mille** (*indeclinable*)	a thousand
minitor, minitari, minitatus sum	I repeatedly threaten
***minor, minari, minatus sum**	I threaten
***minus** (*adverb*)	less
misceo, miscere, miscui, mixtum	I mix, mix in, mingle; I stir up (628), throw into confusion (805); I exchange (720)
***miser, misera, miserum**	wretched, poor
misereor, misereri, miseritus sum (+ *genitive*)	I pity, take pity on
***mitto, mittere, misi, missum**	I send; inflict (629)
***moenia, -ium** *n. pl.*	city walls; city
molior, moliri, molitus sum	I engineer, devise
mollis -is -e	soft, gentle; easy
monimentum, -i *n.*	reminder
***mons, montis** *m.*	mountain
monstrum, -i *n.*	portent; monster, horrible creature; monstrous portent (874)
***mora, -ae** *f.*	delay
***morbus, -i** *m.*	disease
***morior, mori, mortuus sum**	I die
***moror, morari, moratus sum**	I delay; prolong (874)
moror in (+ *ablative*)	I delay over (781)
***mors, mortis** *f.*	death
morsus, -us *m.*	bite; biting grip
mortalis, -is *m.*	a mortal person (850)
mortalis -is -e	mortal; inflicted by a mortal (797)

*mos, moris *m.*	custom; practice
*moveo, movere, movi, motum	I move; I set in motion
mucro, mucronis *m.*	sword-point; sword
mugitus, -us *m.*	bellow
*multi -ae -a	many
*multus -a -um	much; many a (68)
muralis -is -e	used to assault a wall, aimed at walls
murmur, murmuris *n.*	low continuous noise; murmur
murra, -ae *f.*	myrrh; perfume
Murranus, -i *m.*	Murranus
*murus, -i *m.*	wall
musso, mussare, mussavi, mussatum	I murmur, mutter (in discontent or indecision); I wonder grumblingly (657), wonder with murmurs (718)
*muto, mutare, mutavi, mutatum	I change
mutus -a -um	dumb
*nam	for
namque	for
nanciscor, nancisci, nactus sum	I come upon
nata, -ae *f.*	daughter
*nauta, -ae *m.*	sailor
ne (+ *imperative/subjunctive*)	do not (72–3n.)
ne ... neu ...	do not ... nor ...
*ne (+ *subjunctive*)	so that ... not, lest
*-ne	(introduces a question)
*nec	see neque
nec non	and furthermore
*nego, negare, negavi, negatum	I deny, refuse to give (914)
nemus, nemoris *n.*	wood, forest, woodland grove
*neque or nec	and not, nor
nec/neque ... aut ...	neither ... nor ... (764–5, 912)
nec/neque ... nec/neque ...	neither ... nor ...
nequiquam	in vain, without success
nervus, -i *m.*	bow-string
neu or neve	and not, nor
ni	if not, unless
*nihil *n.* (*indeclinable*)	nothing
nihil est quod	there is no reason why (11–12n.)

nitor, niti, nixus sum	I strain, struggle
nivalis -is -e	snowy
nix, nivis *f.*	snow; (pl.) falls or drifts of snow
*nomen, nominis *n.*	name
*non	not
*nos, nostri/nostrum	we, us
nosco, noscere, novi, notum	I recognize
*noster, nostra, nostrum	our; inflicted by us (51)
*notus -a -um	known
*novus -a -um	new; unfamiliar (867)
*Nox, Noctis *f.*	Night (the goddess)
nubes, nubis *f.*	cloud
*nullus -a -um	not any, no
*numerus, -i *m.*	number
*numquam	never
*nunc	now
nunc deinde	from now on, henceforth
*nuntius, -ii *m.*	messenger
nympha, -ae *f.*	nymph
o (*interjection*)	O (19n., 883–4n.)
ob (+ *accusative*)	right in front of
obnitor, obniti, obnixus sum	I push against (105); I strain hard (721)
obscenus -a -um	ill-omened
obstipesco, obstipescere, obstipui	I am struck dumb, am stunned
obtestor, obtestari, obtestatus sum	I beg
obtutus, -us *m.*	fixed gaze
occido, occidere, occidi, occasum	I fall; I die
occulo, occulere, occului, occultum	I hide
occurro, occurrere, occurri, occursum	I rush to confront (854); I counter (625)
ocior	more swift
ocius (*adverb*)	swiftly
*oculus, -i *m.*	eye
*odium, -ii *n.*	hatred
oleaster, oleastri *m.*	a wild olive (tree)
*olim	since long ago (767)
olli	see ille (18n., 788n.)
Olympus, -i *m.*	Olympus

omen, ominis *n.*	omen
omnipotens (*genitive* omnipotentis)	all-powerful
*omnis -is -e	all
oppeto, oppetere, oppeti(v)i, oppetitum	I meet my end, perish
*oppidum, -i *n.*	town
oppono, opponere, opposui, oppositum (+ *dative*)	I put in the way of
me oppono (+ *dative*)	I put myself in the way of
*ops, opis *f.*	support, assistance
opto, optare, optavi, optatum	I wish; I long (to do something)
*opus, operis *n.*	work; (pl.) siege operations (699)
*ora, -ae *f.*	coast; edge (924)
orbis, orbis *m.*	circle; circuit (763); ball (of eye) (670); world (708)
ordior, ordiri, orsus sum	I begin to speak; I speak
orichalcum, -i *n.*	mountain-copper
Orithyia, -ae *f.*	Orithyia
*oro, orare, oravi, oratum	I beg
*os, oris *n.*	mouth; lips (802); voice (692); language (837); face (66, 656, 865, 871)
os, ossis *n.*	bone
ostrum, -i *n.*	crimson
paciscor, pacisci, pactus sum	I barter
Pallas, Pallantis *m.*	Pallas
palma, -ae *f.*	palm (of the hand)
palor, palari, palatus sum	I wander, stray, scatter
palus, paludis *f.*	marsh
pando, pandere, pandi, passum	I open up
pango, pangere, pepigi, pactum	I pledge
*par (*genitive* paris)	equal; similar, matching
paratus -a -um	prepared, ready
*parco, parcere, peperci	I refrain
*parens, parentis *m./f.*	parent; father
*paro, parare, paravi, paratum	I prepare
*pars, partis *f.*	part
Parthus, -i *m.*	a Parthian

partus, -us *m.*	birth, act of giving birth
*parvus -a -um	small
pateo, patere, patui	I lie open
*pater, patris *m.*	father
*patior, pati, passus sum	I endure; I suffer
*patria, -ae *f.*	homeland, fatherland
patrius -a -um	belonging to a father (736); ancestral (834)
*pauci -ae -a	few
pavidus -a -um	frightened
*pax, pacis *f.*	peace, peace settlement
pecto, pectere, pex(u)i, pexum	I comb
pectus, pectoris *n.*	chest, breast; heart
pecus, pecoris *n.*	herd
penes (+ *accusative*)	in the hands of
penna, -ae *f.*	feather (750); wing (892)
*per (+ *accusative*)	through, throughout; by means of (632); (*in oaths*) by (56)
perfero, perferre, pertuli, perlatum	I deliver (a blow), drive home
perfidus -a -um	untrustworthy
*perfundo, perfundere, perfudi, perfusum	I pour over, bathe
*perpetior, perpeti, perpessus sum	I allow, tolerate, endure
*pes, pedis *m.*	foot
pestis, pestis *f.*	destruction; plague; bringer of destruction (845)
*peto, petere, petivi, petitum	I seek, seek out
phalanx, phalangis *f.*	phalanx, battalion
Phrygius -a -um	Phrygian
Phryx, Phrygis *m.*	a Phrygian
pietas, pietatis *f.*	dutifulness
Pilumnus, -i *m.*	Pilumnus
placeo, placere, placui, placitum	I please
plaudo, plaudere, plausi, plausum	I pat
*poena, -ae *f.*	punishment
Poeni, -orum *m. pl.*	the Carthaginians
pondus, ponderis *n.*	weight
*pono, ponere, posui, positum	I place, put in place
*pons, pontis *m.*	bridge

poples, poplitis *m.*	knee
****porta, -ae** f.*	gate
*posco, poscere, poposci	I demand, call for
*possum, posse, potui	I am able
*postquam	after; when
*potens (*genitive* **potentis**)	powerful, mighty
*potior, potiri, potitus sum (+ *ablative*)	I gain possession of; I am in possession of
*potius	rather
praeceps (*genitive* **praecipitis**)	headlong; in a headlong rush
praecipito, praecipitare, praecepi, praeceptum	I throw headlong, throw aside, jettison
*praemium, -ii *n.*	prize, reward
praesens (*genitive* **praesentis**)	present; immediate
praesto, praestare, praestiti	I am outstanding
*praeterea	furthermore
*precor, precari, precatus sum	I pray
premo, premere, pressi, pressum	I press upon
prendo, prendere, prendi, prensum	I catch up with
prex, precis *f.*	prayer
*primus -a -um	first; above all (33); the beginning of (103, 735)
*pro (+ *ablative*)	for, on behalf of, for the sake of; in front of; in return for (878)
probo, probare, probavi, probatum	I authorize
*procul	from a distance
*procurro, procurrere, pro(cu)curri, procursum	I run forward
procursus, -us *m.*	a run forward
procus, -i *m.*	suitor
*prodo, prodere, prodidi, proditum	I betray, abandon
*produco, producere, produxi, productum	I bring forth
*proelium, -ii *n.*	battle
profanus -a -um	not sacred, without sanctity, deconsecrated
proles, prolis *f.*	offspring, child

proludo, proludere, prolusi, prolusum	I practise
proluo, proluere, prolui, prolutum	I wash away the area in front
promissum, -i *n.*	promise
***promitto, promittere, promisi, promissum**	I promise
propago, propaginis *f.*	a plant from which other plants are grown; offspring; race (827)
properus -a -um	acting with haste
***prosequor, prosequi, prosecutus sum**	I follow; I send (someone) on their way
protendo, protendere, protendi, protentum	I stretch forth (930–1n.)
***pudor, pudoris** *m.*	sense of shame
***puer, pueri** *m.*	boy
***pugna, -ae** *f.*	fight, fighting, battle
pugnus, -i *m.*	fist
pulso, pulsare, pulsavi, pulsatum	I batter
pulvis, pulveris *m.*	dust
puniceus -a -um	scarlet
purus -a -um	clear, free from obstructions
***puto, putare, putavi, putatum**	I think
qua (*adverb*)	where
quacumque (*adverb*)	wherever, in whatever manner
***quaero, quaerere, quaesivi, quaesitum**	I seek
quaeso	I ask; please (72–3n.)
***qualis, qualis, quale**	like; such as (900)
***quamquam**	although
***quando**	see **si quando**
quantum	as much as, the more (19–20n.)
***quantus -a -um**	how great, what great; as (701–3n.)
quasso, quassare, quassavi, quassatum	I shake repeatedly
***-que**	and; or (893)
-que . . . -que . . .	both . . . and . . . (833; but see 23n.)
***qui, quae, quod** (*interrogative adjective*)	which, what
***qui, quae, quod** (*relative pronoun*)	who, which

*quia	because
quicumque, quaecumque, quodcumque	whoever, whatever
quid (*adverb*)	why (620, 889)
*quidem	indeed
*quies, quietis *f.*	rest
quiesco, quiescere, quievi, quietum	I rest, am still
*quinque (*indeclinable*)	five
*quis, quid	who, what
*quisquam, quisquam, quicquam	anyone, anything
*quisque, quaeque, quidque	each person, each thing
*quisquis, quisquis, quidquid	anyone who, anything that; whoever, whatever
*quo (*adverb*)	whither, to where; in what direction; to what end, for what purpose (37, 879)
quondam	at times
*quoniam	since
radix, radicis *f.*	root
rapidus -a -um	quick, swift
*rapio, rapere, rapui, raptum	I snatch up
recaleo, recalere	I am hot
*recedo, recedere, recessi, recessum	I withdraw, retire, depart
recludo, recludere, reclusi, reclusum	I open up; I pierce
recumbo, recumbere, recubui	I lie back
recurso, recursare (+ *dative*)	I keep coming back to
recuso, recusare, recusavi, recusatum	I refuse
*reddo, reddere, reddidi, redditum	I give back; I restore; I hand over; I allot (817)
refello, refellere, refelli	I refute
*refero, referre, rettuli, relatum	I carry back; I bear (76); I redirect (657); (passive) I slip backwards (37)
me refero	I make my way back (865–6, see also **fero**)
*reficio, reficere, refeci, refectum	I restore, revive

*refugio, refugere, refugi	I turn back and flee away, I flee back
refuto, refutare, refutavi, refutatum	I prove wrong
*regina, -ae *f.*	queen
*regnum, -i *n.*	kingdom
*rego, regere, rexi, rectum	I rule; I control
*relinquo, relinquere, reliqui, relictum	I leave, leave behind, abandon
remitto, remittere, remisi, remissum	I send back, return (929); I relax
me remitto (*reflexive*)	I relax my attitude (833)
remugio, remugire	I re-echo, resound
repertor, repertoris *m.*	creator
repono, reponere, reposui, repositum	I put (in place of something else)
reposco, reposcere	I demand redemption of
reprimo, reprimere, repressi, repressum	I hold back, check
requies, requietis *f.*	rest, comfort
*res, rei *f.*	thing, matter; (pl.) situation (43, 643, 665)
*respicio, respicere, respexi, respectum	I look back at; I consider (43)
resplendeo, resplendere	I glitter
*respondeo, respondere, respondi, responsum	I reply
responso, responsare	I ring out in answer
resto, restare, restiti	I remain, I am left
retexo, retexere, retexui, retextum	I retrace, I go back over in the reverse direction
retorqueo, retorquere, retorsi, retortum	I twist around
retracto, retractare, retractavi, retractatum	I take back, cancel (11); I hang back (889)
revello, revellere, revelli, revulsum	I tear off, tear out
revincio, revincire, revinxi, revinctum (+ *ablative*)	I gird with
*rex, regis *m.*	king
*ripa, -ae *f.*	riverbank

ritus, -us *m.*	ritual
robur, roboris *n.*	wood
Romanus -a -um	Roman
rosa, -ae *f.*	rose
rota, -ae *f.*	wheel; (pl.) chariot (671)
rubeo, rubere	I blush, redden
ruber, rubra, rubrum	red
rubor, ruboris *m.*	blush
***rumpo, rumpere, rupi, ruptum**	I break, break through; I break off
ruo, ruere, rui	I rush, rush up
***rursus**	again
Rutuli, -orum *m. pl.*	the Rutulians
sacer, sacra, sacrum	sacred, holy
sacra, -orum *n. pl.*	sacred rites
Saces, Sacae *m.*	Saces
saeculum, -i *n.*	age, era
per saecula	throughout the ages, for ever (826)
***saepe**	often
saepio, saepire, saepsi, saeptum	I surround, shut in
***saevus -a -um**	savage, brutal, cruel
sagitta, -ae *f.*	arrow
saltus, -us *m.*	leap
***salus, salutis** *f.*	safety; hope of safety, means of deliverance (653)
sanctus -a -um	holy; pure, blameless (648)
sanguineus -ea -eum	blood-red
***sanguis, sanguinis** *m.*	blood
***satis**	enough, sufficiently
Saturnius -a -um	born of Saturn
Saturnus, -i *m.*	Saturn
satus -a -um (+ *ablative*)	sprung from, begotten of
sata, -ae *f.*	daughter
saucius -a -um	wounded
saxum, -i *n.*	rock
sceleratus -a -um	criminal
scindo, scindere, scicidi/scidi, scissum	I rend, tear
scintilla, -ae *f.*	spark
***scio, scire, sci(v)i, scitum**	I know

*se (*or* sese)	himself, herself, itself, themselves
secum	with himself, herself, itself, themselves; by himself, alone (843)
secus (*adverb*)	differently
*sed	but
sedeo, sedere, sedi, sessum	I sit
*sedes, sedis *f.*	seat
sedo, sedare, sedavi, sedatum	I make calm, becalm
seges, segetis *f.*	crop
segnis -is -e	slow, sluggish
semivir (*genitive* semiviri)	half a man
*semper	always
senecta, -ae *f.*	old age
sensus, -us *m.*	feeling, emotion
septemplex (*genitive* septemplicis)	seven-layered
*sequor, sequi, secutus sum	I follow; I follow (a leader), obey (718); I follow readily (912); I flow out (51); I catch (775–6n.); I head for (893)
sermo, sermonis *m.*	speech (940); language (834)
serpens, serpentis *m./f.*	snake
serus -a -um	late
*servo, servare, servavi, servatum	I save
sese	see **se**
*seu	see **sive**
*sex (*indeclinable*)	six
*si	if
si quando	if ever (749); whenever (851)
si quis	if any
*sic	in this way, thus; in the same way, in the manner just specified (913)
sidus, sideris *n.*	star
significo, significare, significavi, significatum	I make a sign
signo, signare, signavi, signatum	I mark out
Sila, -ae *f.*	Sila
*silva, -ae *f.*	woodland, wood
*similis -is -e	like, looking like

*simul (*adverb*)	at the same time
*sine (+ *ablative*)	without
*sino, sinere, sivi, situm	I allow
*sive or seu	or; or if
seu ... aut ...	whether ... or ...
sive ... sive ...	either ... or ...
socio, sociare, sociavi, sociatum	I join
*socius, -i *m.*	ally
*soleo, solere, solitus sum	I am accustomed
solium, -ii *n.*	throne
solum, -i *n.*	ground
*solus -a -um	alone, on one's own
*solvo, solvere, solvi, solutum	I loosen; I make slack (867, 951)
*somnus, -i *m.*	(sing. or pl.) sleep
sono, sonare, sonui, sonitum	I make a noise; I screech (866)
sonorus -a -um	clanging loudly
*sonus, -i *m.*	sound
*soror, sororis *f.*	sister
sors, sortis *f.*	lot; fortune; circumstances (54)
sortior, sortiri, sortitus sum	I choose
spargo, spargere, sparsi, sparsum	I scatter; I hurl showers of (51)
*spatium, -ii *n.*	space, distance
spatium do	I give way (696)
*specto, spectare, spectavi, spectatum	I watch
*spes, spei *f.*	hope
spira, -ae *f.*	coil
spolio, spoliare, spoliavi, spoliatum	I strip; I rob
*spolium, -ii *n.*	spoil (equipment taken from a defeated enemy)
spondeo, spondere, spopondi, sponsum	I pledge, give an assurance of
spumo, spumare, spumavi, spumatum	I foam
squaleo, squalere, squalui	I am rough, am scaly
sterno, sternere, stravi, stratum	I lay low, lay flat on the ground
stirps, stirpis *m./f.*	trunk (770); stump (781)
*sto, stare, steti, statum	I stand; I come to a standstill (718)

stat (+ _infinitive_)	it is (my) fixed resolve (to do something) (678)
strido, stridere, stridi	I whirr, hum; I whizz
stridor, stridoris _m._	whirring noise
stringo, stringere, strinxi, strictum	I draw (a weapon)
struo, struere, struxi, structum	I arrange; I plot (796)
stupeo, stupere, stupui	I am dumbstruck, stunned, astounded
Stygius -a -um	Stygian, of the Styx
suadeo, suadere, suasi, suasum	I urge, advise
***sub** (+ _ablative_)	under; inside (831, 950); close up to (811)
***sub** (+ _accusative_)	down to
subdo, subdere, subdidi, subditum	I place underneath
***subeo, subire, subi(v)i, subitum**	I come up (733); I go underneath so as to support, I carry (899)
***subicio, subicere, subieci, subiectum**	I throw up, send up
subitus -a -um	sudden
sublabor, sublabi, sublapsus sum	I slip in, creep up
sublimis -is -e	imposingly tall; high-spirited
subrideo, subridere, subrisi, subrisum (+ _dative_)	I smile at, laugh at
subsidium, -ii _n._	aid, help
subsido, subsidere, subsedi	I sink into insignificance
subsisto, subsistere, substiti	I come to a halt
successus, -us _m._	success
***succido, succidere, succidi**	I fall down, collapse
succurro, succurrere, succurri, succursum (+ _dative_)	I go to help
sufficio, sufficere, suffeci, suffectum	I suffice; I am available, present (912)
***sum, esse, fui**	I am
summitto, summittere, summisi, summissum	I lower, cast down, make submissive; moderate (832)
***summus -a -um**	highest; on high; the top of
***sumo, sumere, sumpsi, sumptum**	I take, take up; I exact (949)
superbus -a -um	proud; despotic
***superus -a -um**	situated above

' **superi, -orum** *m. pl.*	the gods above
*__supero, superare, superavi,__	I overcome; I have the upper hand
superatum	(676); I survive (639); I am left,
	remain (873)
superstitio, superstitionis *f.*	object of religious awe
supplex (*genitive* **supplicis**)	begging (for mercy or favour),
	suppliant
supra (+ *accusative*)	beyond
supremus -a -um	last remaining (653)
supremum, -i *n.*	the very end (803)
*__surgo, surgere, surrexi, surrectum__	I rise
suspendo, suspendere, suspendi,	I hang up
suspensum	
sustento, sustentare, sustentavi,	I endure without giving way
sustentatum	
sustineo, sustinere, sustinui	I hold up
*__suus -a -um__	his, her, its, their
tabulatum, -i *n.*	floor, storey, level
Taburnus, -i *m.*	Taburnus
*__tacitus -a -um__	silent
*__talis -is -e__	such, of such a kind; in such a
	manner (860)
*__tamen__	however
*__tandem__	at last; (*with imperative*) really, for
	the last time
*__tango, tangere, tetigi, tactum__	I touch; I affect with emotion, move
	(933)
tanto	so much, the more (20–1n.)
*__tantum, -i__ *n.*	(*as pronoun*) so much, this much
	and no more (885n.)
	(*accusative used adverbially*) only
	(835)
*__tantus -a -um__	so great, such great (cf. 72n.)
tardo, tardare, tardavi, tardatum	I cause to slow down
Tartara, -orum *n. pl.*	Tartarus
Tartareus -a -um	dwelling in Tartarus
taurus, -i *m.*	bull
*__tectum, -i__ *n.*	building
*__tego, tegere, texi, tectum__	I cover, conceal

tellus, telluris *f.*	earth
*telum, -i *n.*	spear (775–6n.); weapon; missile (858), arrow (815)
tempto, temptare, temptavi, temptatum	I try, attempt
*tempus, temporis *n.*	time
tendo, tendere, tetendi, tentum/tensum	I stretch; I stretch out (936); I proceed (917), press on (in an attitude) (938)
*teneo, tenere, tenui, tentum	I hold; I take hold of; I hold on to (834); I hold fast (773, 778); I bind (819)
*tergum, tergi *n.*	back
terga do	I turn tail
*Terra, -ae *f.*	Earth (the goddess)
*terra, -ae *f.*	land
*terreo, terrere, terrui, territum	I frighten, terrify
terribilis -is -e	frightening
terrificus -a -um	terrifying
territo, territare, territavi	I terrify
*terror, terroris *m.*	terror
tete	see **tu**
Teucrus -a -um	Teucrian, Trojan (60n.)
Teucri, -orum *m. pl.*	the Trojans
Thybrinus -a -um	of the Tiber
*timeo, timere, timui	I fear, am afraid
tingo, tingere, tinxi, tinctum	I plunge, dip
*tollo, tollere, sustuli, sublatum	I raise, lift up; I remove; I put an end to (39)
tono, tonare, tonui	I thunder; I rumble
tormentum, -i *n.*	war-machine (for discharging missiles)
torpor, torporis *m.*	numbness
torqueo, torquere, torsi, tortum	I twist, turn; I shoot (858), send spinning (901)
torus, -i *m.*	muscle (6–7n.)
totidem (*indeclinable adjective*)	the same number of
totiens	so often
*totus -a -um	whole

trabs, trabis *f.*	timber, beam of wood
***traho, trahere, traxi, tractum**	I drag
***transeo, transire, transi(v)i,** **transitum**	I pass through, pierce
transilio, transilire, transilui	I leap through
tremesco, tremescere	I tremble
tremo, tremere, tremui	I tremble, quiver
trepido, trepidare, trepidavi, **trepidatum**	I am agitated
trepidus -a -um	agitated; hasty
***tristis -is -e**	sad; bitter
Troia, -ae *f.*	Troy
Troianus -a -um	Trojan
Troiani, -orum *m. pl.*	the Trojans
Troiugena, -ae *m.*	a man from Troy, a Trojan
Tros (*adjective*)	Trojan
Troes, Troum *m. pl.*	the Trojans
truncus, -i *m.*	trunk
***tu, tui**	you (singular)
tete	= **te** (accusative singular of **tu**)
tueor, tueri	I see, look; I watch; I guard (34)
***tum**	then; moreover (906)
tum demum	only then
***tumultus, -us** *m.*	uproar
turbidus -a -um	agitated; wild
turbo, turbare, turbavi, turbatum	I agitate (70); I stir up, make turbulent (620); I disrupt (633)
turbo, turbinis *m.*	whirling motion, spinning motion (855); whirlwind (923); force
Turnus, -i *m.*	Turnus
turris, turris *f.*	tower
***tuus -a -um**	your
tyrannus, -i *m.*	tyrant
***ubi**	when; where
Ufens, Ufentis *m.*	Ufens
***ullus -a -um**	any
ulterior -ior -ius	further
ultro (*adverb*)	without hesitation (3n.)
Umber, Umbra, Umbrum	Umbrian, from Umbria

Umber, Umbri *m.*	Umbrian dog (753n.)
umbra, -ae *f.*	shadow, shade; (sing. or pl.) darkness; (pl.) the underworld (881, 952)
umerus, -i *m.*	shoulder
***umquam**	ever
***unda, -ae** *f.*	wave; river, body of water; water
***undique**	on all sides
undo, undare, undavi, undatum	I billow
unguis, unguis *m.*	nail (on finger)
***unus -a -um**	one
***urbs, urbis** *f.*	city
urgeo, urgere, ursi	I press hard (in pursuit)
usquam	anywhere
usque adeo	to so great an extent
***ut**	(+ *subjunctive*) so that, in order that; that
	(+ *indicative*) when; as
ut primum	as soon as
***utor, uti, usus sum** (+ *ablative*)	I use; I make use of, exploit (932)
utrimque	on both sides
vacuus -a -um	empty
***valeo, valere, valui, valitum**	I am strong; I have power; I am able
***validus -a -um**	strong, mighty
vanus -a -um	empty
varius -a -um	changing; complex; of many kinds
vastus -a -um	huge; desolate
***-ve**	or; and (621n.)
***veho, vehere, vexi, vectum**	I carry
***vel**	or
***velut** or **veluti**	just as
venator, venatoris *m.*	hunter (but see 751n.)
venenum, -i *n.*	poison
venerabilis -is -e	worthy of reverence
***venio, venire, veni, ventum**	I come
venor, venari, venatus sum	I hunt
ventosus -a -um	swift as the wind
***ventus, -i** *m.*	wind
Venus, Veneris *f.*	Venus

verber, verberis *n.*	beat; (pl.) beating
***verbum, -i** *n.*	word
vergo, vergere	I sink down
***vero**	truly
verso, versare, versavi, versatum	I keep turning; I drive around
vertex, verticis *m.*	whirling column (673); peak, summit (684, 703)
***verto, vertere, verti, versum**	I change, alter, turn; (passive) I go to and fro, whirl around (915)
verum	but
***verus -a -um**	true; just (694)
***vester, vestra, vestrum**	belonging to you (plural), your
***vestis, -is** *f.*	clothing; (pl.) garments
***veto, vetare, vetui, vetitum**	I forbid
***vetus** (*genitive* **veteris**)	old, ancient
vetustas, vetustatis *f.*	age, old age
***via, -ae** *f.*	road, way; way (of doing something)
vibro, vibrare, vibravi, vibratum	I curl, crimp
***victoria, -ae** *f.*	victory
***video, videre, vidi, visum**	I see; I observe; I perceive (with the mind)
***videor, videri, visus sum**	I seem
vinclum, -i *n.*	bond
***vinco, vincere, vici, victum**	I conquer, overcome, win over
violentia, -ae *f.*	violent passion
violo, violare, violavi, violatum	I defile, stain (67); I violate (797)
***vir, viri** *m.*	man
virginitas, virginitatis *f.*	virginity
virgo, virginis *f.*	maiden
***virtus, virtutis** *f.*	bravery, courage, valour
***vis** (*accusative* **vim**, *ablative* **vi**) *f.*	force; (pl.: **vires, virium**) physical strength
***vita, -ae** *f.*	life
vividus -a -um	vigorous
***vix**	scarcely, only just
vocatus, -us *m.*	call, summoning, summons
vociferor, vociferari, vociferatus sum	I cry aloud

*voco, vocare, vocavi, vocatum I call; I call out for (780); I call by a name, designate (658, 824)

Volcanius -a -um manufactured by Vulcan

*volo, velle, volui I want

volo, volare, volavi, volatum I fly; I hurry

volucris, volucris *f.* bird

voluntas, voluntatis *f.* will; goodwill

voluto, volutare, volutavi, volutatum I turn over in my mind

volvo, volvere, volvi, volutum I cause to roll, send rolling (906); I turn over in my mind (831); I roll (my eyes), cause (my eyes) to travel restlessly (939); (passive, in middle sense) I roll (672)

*vos, vestri/vestrum you (plural)

votum, -i *n.* prayer

voveo, vovere, vovi, votum I vow

*vox, vocis *f.* voice, call; utterance; sound, cry (929); language, speech (825)

*vulnus, -eris *n.* wound

*vultus, -us *m.* face; expression